INCIDENTS

OF A

SOUTHERN TOUR:

OR

THE SOUTH,

AS SEEN WITH NORTHERN EYES.

BY REV. H. COWLES ATWATER, A. M.

"'Tis hard to leave the South's inspiring sky,
From orange groves and spicy gales to fly;
To look on nature in her brightest dress,
Nor heave a sigh for her lost loveliness."

BOSTON:
J. P. MAGEE, No. 5, CORNHILL.

1857

The noble horse,
That, in his fiery youth, from his wide nostrils
Neighed courage to his rider, and brake through
Groves of opposed pikes, bearing his lord
Safe to triumphant victory, old or wounded,
Was set at liberty, and freed from service.
The Athenian mules, that from the quarry drew
Marble, hewed for the Temple of the Gods,
The great work ended, were dismissed and fed
At the public cost; nay, faithful dogs have found
Their sepulchres; but man, to man more cruel,
Appoints no end to the sufferings of his slave.

MASSINGER.

INDEX.

CHAPTER XII.

CHAPTER XIII.

CHAPTER XIV.

CHAPTER XV.

CHAPTER XVI.

CHAPTER XVII.

CHAPTER XVIII.

THE WARNING.

"BEWARE! The Israelite of old, who tore
 The lion in his path.—when, poor and blind,
He saw the blessed light of heaven no more,
 Shorn of his noble strength and forced to grind
In prison, and at last led forth to be
A pander to Philistine revelry,—

Upon the pillars of the temple laid
 His desperate hands, and in its overthrow
Destroyed himself, and with him those who made
 A cruel mockery of his sightless woe;
The poor, blind Slave, the scoff and jest of all,
Expired, and thousands perished in the fall!

There is a poor, blind Samson in this land,
 Shorn of his strength, and bound in bonds of steel,
Who may, in some grim revel, raise his hand,
 And shake the pillars of this Commonweal,
Till the vast Temple of our liberties
A shapeless mass of wreck and rubbish lies."

INTRODUCTION.

PROBABLY no one will deny that the question now most emphatically before the American people, is that of Slavery in its different aspects. Shall it become one of our permanent and highly cherished institutions, growing with our growth, and strengthening with our strength, expanding with every acre of annexed territory, or shall it be circumscribed, till it starves itself to death? Since the formation of the Federal Union, no question of such vital importance in morals, or political economy, has so deeply stirred and moved the hearts of the people. Conferences, Associations, General Assemblies, organizations composed of those whose mission it is to proclaim, "Peace on earth and good will towards men," have been torn assunder by it.

The excitement which has been, is as nothing (we believe) in comparison with that, which is to be, *and must be*, before the question is settled.

And the future must reveal whether there is strength enough in the Union to abide this internal pressure, this conflict of opinion.

It is a Moral, a Political, and Pecuniary question. In one or the other of these aspects, it reaches every person in the community.

No one can have marked the rise, and increasing interest which gathers around this question, without being convinced, that neither party will, "conquer their prejudices." But the conflict between these two opposing principles, Freedom and Slavery, Civilization and Barbarism, must go on, whatever be the consequences, till one or the other bites the dust.

It is not the special object of these pages, to argue this great question, either pro or con.

This has been already done, by some of the ablest pens our country affords.

I desire to describe to the reader, as best I may, scenes that were witnessed during a pleasant sojourn in that land of sunshine and song, of birds and flowers, and in many instances, of large hearted hospitality, as well as the impression that those scenes made on my mind. There is much ignorance in the Free States, of the true condition of things at the South. This results from various causes. One cause may be, the perusing the works of superficial observers. A "South Side view of three months," will be most emphatically, *a South Side view.* The charm and the novelty of ones situation, does not wear off in that time, especially if our intercourse is with the hospitable planters. It needs a longer residence, and more extended opportunities for observation, to take the true measure of the blessings, as well as of the woes and sorrows of the system, than many writers have enjoyed.

The author flatters himself that few ever had better opportunities for looking at the subject. Though he is deeply conscious of not being able to describe what he saw, with that life-like and graphic power so necessary in word painting.

A few, only, of many, "Incidents," are here presented to the reader. Others are reserved for a more permanent volume.

If the facts here delineated, should enable the reader to obtain a more just idea of what Slavery is, and of its influence upon the community who tolerate it, I shall not have used my pen in vain.

THE AUTHOR.

INCIDENTS OF A SOUTHERN TOUR.

CHAPTER I.

CLIMATE OF THE SOUTH.

FROM October till April, I can testify from experience, it is all that heart can wish. It is just that medium between heat and cold, that makes it the joy of one's life to be abroad in the open air. Out in the glorious sunlight, where God intended we should be, if we would enjoy health; rather than within, breathing the vitiated air of our close rooms, as is the custom with but too many, in our bleak New England clime.

They have not to wage a fierce and unequal war, during half the year, as we, with storm and tempest, —rain, hail and snow, when all the treasures of the frozen north are being poured out—coming richly freighted with rheumatic pains, influenzas, colds, consumption and death. It is but the sad experience of too many, that the hard earnings of six months are all consumed, in furnishing a warm habitation, clothing, and fuel, to keep them comfortable during the other six.

All this extra expense is saved in that more favored clime.

2A

Months of their winter weather, might be compared to the few days of our Indian Summer—the crown that Autumn puts on, ere she resigns her sceptre.

Nor after diligent inquiry, did we find one to complain of that heat, which so many suppose, makes the South first cousin to the torrid zone.

Those extremes of heat and cold, which we must endure, and which are so fatal to health, are there unknown.

The thermometer here, as we know from experience, often ranging from forty to fifty degrees in twenty-four hours.

No wonder that such changes, bring thousands each year to a premature grave.

As we breathed their atmosphere, so soft, grateful and healing to the lungs, as though manufactured to order, of etherial oil; and walked in the shade of water oaks, the China tree and splendid magnolias, at a time, when stern winter was holding her iron sway over the entire North, spreading ruin, desolation, and suffering far and wide. We were led to doubt, whether God ever intended this northern region to be inhabited.

And we saw new reason for admiring the energy and perseverence, found among the free born sons of New England, that in spite of our rocky, sterile soil, and bleak clime, had enabled them to build so many great cities, cover the land with smiling villages, erecting so many monuments to learning and the arts.

Let but the curse of Slavery be removed from the South, and free labor develop her resources, she would enter upon a career of prosperity, which would change her present wilderness appearance, into a well watered garden of beauty, fertility and profit.

The South is the land of fruits and flowers, sunshine, and song. From July till December, the most delicious peaches are ripening. Figs abound, of a flavor so rich—that when once eaten, they can never be forgotten. June, the month of roses with us, flies quickly past, and leaves only a pleasant memory of itself.

But there, this queen of flowers may be almost said to sway her sceptre for the entire year. In the beautiful city of Vicksburg, in November, the sidewalk was literally strewed with roses, which, in trimming away the luxuriant growth, had been cut off, and thrown into the street. In Natches, at Christmas, the finest and fairest of flowers were blooming, as if awaiting the hand of beauty, to weave them into crowns and chaplets, fit ornaments for the temple of the living God.

The grounds of a gentleman, whose hospitalities I enjoyed, were adorned with more than one hundred varieties of roses, with an uncounted number of other beautiful flowers, easily cultivated in that clime, where winter is unknown. But which few northern eyes are allowed to rejoice in the beholding.

At Baton Rouge, the Capital of Louisiana, on the first Sabbath of the new year, one of the fair worshipers brought and placed upon the communion table, in front of me, a splendid boquet of flowers, gathered fresh from the garden. And, certainly, it would take a sterner Puritan than myself, to condemn or declare out of taste or place—the beautiful, the fragrant offering. Nor would we dare deny, but that some of the inspiration of the hour, was derived from that splendid gift.

CHAPTER II.

FAIRY LAND.

PROBABLY no where in America, will a scene of more quiet beauty be presented to the eye of the traveler, than is witnessed on the Mississippi for one hundred miles above New Orleans; extending also below the city, towards the Balize. For richness and fertility, this is the garden of the world. Man cannot tell, for how many years the Mississippi, and its tributaries have been bringing down, and silently depositing in this extensive Delta, a soil, which seems to have almost fabulous powers of reproduction.

Those magnificent Bluffs, which give such an air of romance to the Upper Mississippi, looking in the distance, like the ruins of old German castles on the Rhine, and which, though decreasing in size, yet have attended the traveler for nearly two thousand miles from the Falls of St. Anthony, have now entirely disappeared. Those vast forests, through which you have been steaming for a thousand miles below St. Louis, no longer line the banks. Every rood of land appears to be under cultivation.

This mighty river, almost the largest in the world, draining well nigh a continent, bearing on its bosom the products of all lands, is sweeping with resistless power, onwards towards the sea. To rescue the soil from an annual overflow, the inhabitants, at great expense, have built a levee, from five to twenty feet high. While the overflow of the Nile brings wealth and a harvest to the Egyptians, the same thing, in respect to the Mississippi, would only bring ruin and destruction. By thus restraining the river, it is higher than the surrounding country.

Every plantation fronts on the river, and extends back, according to circumstances. The public road, on each side, is just within the levee. And near it, stands the mansion of the proprietor, almost smothered in a grove of orange, lemon and citron trees, laden with their golden fruit, together with roses; and myrtles, laurels, cape jessamines and oleanders, while the splendid magnolia, the China, tree and water oak, scattered thickly around, give an air of beauty and grandeur to the scene, that once beheld, is never forgotten. Nestling in the same shade, are the long rows of the white-washed cottages of his "people." But a little distance removed, is the sugar-house, from whose tall chimney stack, a dense volume of smoke is continually ascending. It is the grinding season; and everywhere is life and activity. No one seems to be idle. There may be seen an army of blacks, with their bright knives flashing in the sunlight, hewing their way steadily through that forest of green cane—that seems to be impenetrable.

Everywhere are teams hurrying to the field, or more slowly returning, laden with that, which is soon to be converted into an article, most indispensible for the pumpkin pies and gingerbread—so esteemed by the Universal Yankee Nation. The merry voices of black and white children, joined with the feathered songsters of the groves, fill the air with melody. At night, the songs of the laborers in the sugar-houses, softened by the distance, borne to us over the water, produces a most charming effect. Back in the rear, as a fit setting or frame work for this beautiful picture, are the ancient forests, composed of trees of gigantic size—magnolias with their glossy emerald leaves, cypresses, live oaks, cotton wood, &c., covered with the most luxuriant supply of the tillyndria, or moss of that Southern clime, trailing from limb to limb, and from tree to tree, glistening in the sunlight, as though just dipped in melted silver. This moss, hanging in folds and streamers from every bough, and moved by every breeze, is, to a northern eye, a very striking object, giving the appearance of woods dressed up for some grand festive occasion.

Then over this industrial, quiet scene of Arcadian beauty, the golden sunlinght is streaming, producing an atmosphere, which the Italians themselves might envy, throwing its robes of crimson and violet, of purple and emerald, over garden and meadow, cane field and orange grove, making that full effluence.

> " That tide of glory which no rest doth know,
> But ever rolls and ever flows."

As though moving through air, from the splendid saloon of the steamer, as she passes from side to side of that noble river, to receive or discharge passengers and freight, the enraptured traveler looks down upon that scene of quiet beauty, as upon some fairy land. So different is the landscape from anything witnessed in his cold northern home, that he can hardly realize, that this is a part of,

> " His own, his native land ! "

CHAPTER III.

HOSPITALITY OF THE SOUTH.

We have most of us heard this lauded to the skies. However great it may be, we do not think the East, North, or West will suffer by the comparison. In forming a right judgment on this matter, we are to take into consideration the different circumstances of the case.

In the Free States, in tens of thousands of instances, the wife and daughters do the whole work, have the entire charge of the family, with no hired servants.

Every guest, from one to ten, is so much additional labor—which they cheerfully perform, and thus give their friends a *practical proof*, that they are welcome. At the South, all this is done by servants. The number of guests does not add so directly to the cares and labors of the mistress, as in the former case. Then, they are very much isolated. On their lone plantations, five or ten miles apart, they see, comparatively, but little company.

The coming of one from the world outside, to relieve the tedium and monotony of their life, is a most welcome event. The planter has leisure. He is glad to have some one come to ride, hunt, fish, and smoke with him.

And the ladies of the family, are glad to have some one to converse with, besides their servants. It is a still and quiet life they lead, on those great plantations, surrounded with the ancient forests—not a house in sight.

The passing of one carriage, horse, or footman, during the day, would be a great event.

The difference in this respect, between the active, bustling, running to and fro in the free states, and the death like silence and inactivity that reigns there, strikes a stranger, as impressively as almost any thing else.

In what free state would one have met with the following treatment? Not far from aristocratic Camden, in South Corolina, after a weary day's travel—the last half in a severe storm—at dusk, I knocked at a planter's door to seek shelter. A tall, lean, lank specimen of humanity appeared. I told him I was sorry to trouble him, but the circumstances of the case rendered it necessary, that I should seek shelter some where, and that I should be satisfied with "common doings and plain fixings"—in short, would make them as little trouble as possible.

He began to walk up and down the piazza with heavy tread, and his shaggy brows seemed to grow darker. He evidently was not in a very hospitable mood. He began to mutter about its not being a very pleasant thing to take in strangers. That one did not know who they were entertaining under such circumstances. Then he would look out into the darkness, which was every moment growing more intense, and at the rain, which was falling as if another flood was coming. I saw it was a desperate case, and that all the eloquence I was master of, must be employed. After further appeals to his better feelings, he yielded, and said that owing to the severity of the storm, he would depart from his usual custom and give me shelter.

He invited me in, and asked if his servants should provide supper, saying, they had finished their meal some time since. But, considering my reception at the door, I told them it was not necessary. We passed a pleasant evening around the cheerful fire, in conversation. Was furnished with a good bed; a fine breakfast was provided me in the morning, and, though the rain still continued, I told mine host that, perhaps, I had better start upon my journey. He gave no invitation to tarry till the weather should be more favorable; and as I parted with him on the piazza, he gave me to understand, that the storm, alone, procured me shelter at his hands the previous night.

Through deep mud and heavy showers, all that day, I passed onward. About four o'clock in the afternoon, the rain pouring faster, and so weary as hardly to be able to put one foot before the other, I turned aside to the fine looking negro quarters of a splendid plantation, and entered the driver's large house, at the same time with himself, as he rode up from a hunting excursion.

After resting and drying myself, it being near sunset, I felt that it would be unpleasant to be caught, as I was the night before, and asked the gentleman if I could tarry with him, using the kitchen floor for my bed, and the fire to keep me warm. He said, "No. That there was a tavern three miles ahead, and I had better go on." It was in vain that I told him of my weary walk; that in the dark, I might not be able to follow the direction to the tavern; that the storm was severe, and that there was danger I might perish in the woods. But I had a harder customer to deal with, than the previous night. Nothing would avail, but I must move on.

I started, and was fortunate enough, late in the evening, to bring up at one of the finest travelers' homes that it was my lot to find in the whole south. Except, for the appearance of a few slaves, I should have fancied myself in one of our most intelligent,

New England families. While supper was preparing, I related to the lady of the house, my treatment a few miles back. That, tired as I was, and in that terrible storm, a gentleman had refused me the privilege of sleeping on his floor. That in six thousand miles travel, in nearly all the States, I had not met such treatment.

After using nearly all the proper adjectives, that memory could call up, to express my indignation at such treatment, she asked me to describe the plantation, and, after I had done so, she startled me, by coolly saying, "It was her honored son in law, who had thus treated me."

I had gone too far to retreat. We had a hearty laugh over the matter. She excused him as well as she could. And such was the excellence of her coffee, bacon, eggs, and other "fixings," with a clean bed and room, that I forgave all; and only wished, if the married daughter was like the mother, that she might have been more fortunate in the choice of a husband.

CHAPTER IV.

GENERAL APPEARANCE OF THE SLAVES.

If there are any left in the Free States, so verdant, as one sometime since confessed he was, as to suppose, that those in bondage, never smile, have no moments of joy and gladness—when they bid dull care begone, if he thinks to see the word " *Slave* " daguerreotyped upon the countenance, in unmistakable characters of the deepest sorrow, " indented on the faces, limbs and actions of the bondmen," he will be most surely disappointed on going South.

Such a person has evidently much to learn of human nature, and with what mighty power of endurance, under adverse circumstances, God hath imbued the heart of man,—a power to make the best of the present, however sad, and,

> " Hope for brighter days,
> Though they should never be."

There is many a one, that has a heart like, Mark Tapley, to " come out strong under adverse circumstances," and actually accomplishes it. They are " jolly " under circumstances so disheartening, that we fear Mark Tapley, even, would have failed.

And probably, there are more of this class, among the African race, than any other. For their inheritance, God gave them a land of sunshine and song. Where it is one eternal spring, and the flowers never fade.

The earth produces almost spontaneously enough to supply his wants. As a race, they are extremely sensitive, being the true children of the sun; and living constantly in the open air, they drink in bright influences from sunshine and flowers, and every thing that is beautiful in earth or sky.

They are easily excited. The slightest thing exalts them to a heaven of rapture, or plunges them into an abyss of grief. In the grateful shade of their own Palms, they lead a careless, happy life, full of mirth, and dance, and song. There, in many a sylvan glade, may be witnessed scenes, that would delight the imagination of a pastoral poet. They have naturally a passionate love for music, which the sorrows of Slavery have not been able to eradicate.

As the boat glides along their rivers and quiet lagoons, with a music surpassing that of the far-famed Gondoliers of Venice, the oarsmen keep time, with a rising and falling strain. Thus, every where, in the boat, or bamboo hut, in every scene of gladness, or grief, at wedding, funeral or religious service, their hearts find vent in song.

The negro has not, like those races who are less favored with climate, to wage a continual war with the elements, and be ever on the alert, lest destruction come upon him.

Such being his antecedents, what wonder, even, with the burden of Slavery upon his shoulders, that he walks the earth with less of care upon his countenance, than we might, at first, imagine. But suppose that he, of all other races, is the least restive, and chafes less, under his galling fetters, it does not afford the slightest justification for placing them upon him.

To one, having a just regard for the rights of man, and reasoning correctly, he will hate Slavery none the less, because now and then, a smile, a gleam of sunshine, flashes over the face of the poor bondman.

The Slave is something of a philosopher ; he knows that there is no help for him,—that " on the side of their oppressors there was *power*." He therefore, wisely resolves, to make the best of his condition, to extract what of happiness he can, from his circumstances, and think as little of the future as possible.

The casual remark made to me in South Carolina, by a very intelligent female slave, as at sunset, with a heavy hoe upon her shoulder, she was passing to the, " Quarters," from the cotton field, doubtless expresses the feelings of thousands,—

" We, in this country, are nothing more than dogs under white people's feet. What use to think? Can't do any thing. No help. Might as well not think." And on she went, humming some negro melody.

The human heart, is a harp of a thousand strings ; and while one is breaking, with the weight of sorrow resting on it, and tears are coursing down the face, by touching another, a gleam of sunshine shall pass o'er it, and the countenance be wreathed with smiles.

The negro is doubtless freed from that carking care and anxiety, which furrows the face of many an Anglo Saxon, and leads him to become prematurely old. Yet, what wise person would say, that for this, his lot was desirable.

Again, perhaps, in no part of America, is there so much in the external world, that is lovely and beautiful, which would tend to beguile the hours of weary labor, as in the slave holding States. Winter is unknown ; flowers ever bloom ; and the woods and fields are vocal with the song of birds from one year's end to the other. And the glory of the evening hour, when the sun sinks to rest, in the azure west, with all the drapery of his clouds about him, tinged with crimson, with purple and gold, equals any thing to be seen in the land of the Orient.

I have seen "Negro Quarters," so picturesquely located, among grand old trees, sycamores, live oaks, cypresses, pines,—the graceful magnolias, with their large oval leaves, so highly polished, and of the richest emerald green, where all that is to be desired in respect to light and shade, shelter, coolness, freshness, is most profusely furnished; and ever and anon, does the restless air fill the whole space between heaven and earth with melody, as it puts myriads of tongues in motion, causing them to babble of pleasant things, and sing songs of a land, where tears are unknown, bringing on their ærial wings, dreams so sweet, so soft, so soothing, that the one most faint and weary, easily sinks to slumber. As I have looked upon such scenes, I have almost wished one of those cabins for my residence.

I have seen Cane fields surrounded with that most beautiful of all hedges, the Cherokee rose, thickly sprinkled with flowers, of the most pearly whiteness. Mocking birds, from early dawn till late at eve, filling the air with melody; while a sunshine more rich and genial, than that which glows on northern hills, or kisses the flowers to life in our sun-lit vallies, is like a sea of glory, every where diffused. While I looked upon those beautiful pictures, I realized that though the toil of the slave was severe, yet the place, and its surroundings, seemed next to Paradise.

The fashionable northern tourist, passing from one southern city to the other, having constantly the well fed and dressed house servants before his eyes, has about as true an idea of the sufferings of Slavery, as the southern traveler would obtain, of the wretchedness of those, who inhabit the cellars and garrets of New York, by promenading, during the pleasant part of the day, several times up and down Broadway.

But a certain writer, of some note, who has apologized for Slavery, thinks because we see not a,"cowed," haggard look on every slave, it must be, that what we read about the horrors of the system, is all poetry, or moon shine.

Will he tell us, how men are able to sleep, the night before their execution? Or how the murderer of Parkman, after a trial of the deepest interest, had, so sadly, to him, closed late at night, with the verdict of guilty, that he could so carelessly tell the jailor to see that a good dinner of roast turkey was provided for him on the morrow, with a due supply of the finest Havanna cigars. One might reasonably have supposed, that with the skeleton figure of the gallows, looming up but a little distance before him, all desire for food or sleep would have left him, for at least, twenty-four hours.

Will the same person explain, by what principles of mental philosophy it was, that in 1855, in Lafayette, Indiana, when three men were to be hung between one and two o'clock, P. M., they should be able to eat a hearty dinner at twelve, saying, that they were not going to die hungry. Then dressed themselves with the greatest care, expending any amount of jokes and witticisms about their death, and its manner, which was so near?

Verily, the human heart is a strange enigma!

CHAPTER V.

THE DRESS OF THE SLAVE.

In traveling, the dress of those we meet is one of the first things that arrests the attention. And from it, we are apt to form some opinion of the character of persons ; of their employment, or standing in society. This is by no means an infallible criterion for forming a judgment, but it necessarily has its effect—the same as the general expression of the countenance.

Probably, in no part of the world—certainly not in America—will one find that general attention to neatness and cleanliness in dress, whether of the laboring class or otherwise, which we see in New England. Our railroad cars, thronged daily with passengers, present the appearance of persons arrayed for some festal occasion, instead of being—as it is—their ordinary traveling attire. The contrast with some parts of the country is most striking. When operatives are dressed in squalor and rags, we at once receive the impression that their lot is one of great hardship ; and when the opposite is true, it gives a favorable impression of their condition.

From the dress of the slaves, what idea would one form of the institution of slavery, is a very natural inquiry.

It would seem, as if some at the north supposed, that every slave wore a kind of state prison garb, by which he might be distinguished at once, from the free black, and his condition read by every eye.

The author of, " A south side view of slavery,"

belongs to this class. Hear him: "To see slaves with broadcloth suits, well fitting;—fine shirts nicely ironed, polished boots, gloves, umbrellas for sun shades, the best of hats, young men with their blue coats and bright buttons, white marseilles vests, white pantaloons, all in the latest style; broaches in their shirt bosoms, gold chains, elegant sticks, and some old men leaning on their ivory headed staves, as respectable in their attire as any others, was more than I was prepared to see." And if he witnessed, what I often did, he might have described colored ladies arrayed in the richest silks; a bonnet and plume that a New York Belle might envy; a Canton crape shawl, of dazzling whiteness, with jewelry and other, "fixings," to match. Perhaps the doctor's wife herself, would hardly present a more dashing or showy appearance.

Certainly, so far as the dress of their house servants is concerned, and many others, in their chief cities, the traveler would see nothing so very objectionable in the system of slavery. By their dress, whether on the sabbath, or at other times, the free black and the slave, could not be distinguished.

That human nature, which leads the northern aristocrat, to furnish white kids to his coachman, and to have all his servants, that his company will be likely to see, dressed with taste, leads the southern gentleman, to be equally liberal in furnishing the wardrobe of those, that are more immediately about his person. The expenditures in this way, besides gratifying his own artistic taste for the beautiful, and being a just reward for meritorious conduct, will tend to give his neighbors a higher opinion of the depth of his purse. But if this gentleman, who, with so much of complacency, calls the attention of his guest to the dress of his servants, would only take him out into the country, to his cotton, rice, or sugar plantation,—or that of his neighbor,—and parade the operatives before him, that vision of neatness, taste, and beauty, would at once be dissolved. And we are to remember, that the dwellers on the plantations are the *many*, and those in the city the *few*. But a short time intervened between a visit to the wild Indians of the Upper Mississippi and its tributaries, and the plantations on the Mexican Gulf, and certainly, we saw little to choose, between the dress of the Indian, and the plantation slave.

The city slave holder, was ever ready to call our attention to the well dressed slaves that thronged the streets, as if this care for the body, would be a sufficient atonement, for putting out the eyes of the soul, leaving that unclothed, shutting and guarding with Argus vigilence, all those avenues which lead to the inexhaustable fountains of knowledge; or the depriving him of his wife and children at pleasure, selling either in the market like a beast, to suit the convenience of another.

The author of, "South side view," seems to have been "carried away with their dissimulation." That he saw so many well dressed—like the beast for the sacrifice on heathen altars—seems to have been a shield so broad, as to hide all the enormities of the system. He says: "Then I fell into some reflections upon the philosophy of dress, as a powerful means of securing respect, and thought how impossible it must soon become, to treat with indignity men who respect themselves, as these men evidently did. Nay, rather, how impossible it clearly was for masters, who could so clothe their servants, to treat them as cattle." And in different ways, with the greatest complacency, he refers to this matter of dress again and again.

But if, instead of spending *three months* at the South, and glancing at the institution from one or two favorable stand points, he had taken a more comprehensive view, and surveyed the country in its length and breadth—had sounded down to the depths of sorrow, covered by that fair exterior—which so held his attention that he looked no farther—he would have come to very different conclusions. He would have seen, as I did, men dressed, as he so graphically describes, standing on the auction block, with the loud voiced auctioneer crying—

"One thousand dollars bid! Who bids higher? One thonsand dollars only—do I hear no more? One thousand dollars, for that splendid specimen of bone and muscle. Examine him, gentlemen, if you please. His back is unscarred; sold for no fault; title good; do I hear no more? Why, gentlemen, he ought to bring at least fifteen hundred dollars. Ten hundred —fifty, I hear—just in time; going! going!—do I hear no more? Going! going! gone!—Step down, boy, there is your master."

Furthermore, Dr. Adams might have seen ladies, as fair as any that promenade Washington street, with the same fashionable style of dress, flounced skirts, flowing sleeves, embroidered bosoms, hair trimmed with ribbons, &c.,—nothing lacking to make them look attractive, in the full flush of their maiden beauty, placed upon the auction block, surrounded by a crowd of lecherous men, each anxious to obtain the prize. And now a deed of shame is enacted that the sun might blush to look upon. My pen cannot describe it. If we had stumbled upon it in some dark corner of the Orient—in grand Cairo, or in Constantinople, it would not be so surprising. But the wonder is, that in free and *Christian* America, such scenes should be matters of every day occurrence.

The bidding is most spirited. By fifties and by hundreds, with gracious smiles and nods on every side, the auctioneer mounts rapidly upwards. When the first excitement of bidding had somewhat subsided, the auctioneer ordered a passage way to be opened through the dense crowd, to the back part of the building. Then the girl must descend from the block, and walk up and down that terrible path—that they might raise their bids, by a nearer view of her beauty. Each one along the line, might stop her, asking any indecent question that his foul heart might prompt, and make such physical examinations as he might choose.

Walking such an avenue, under such terrible circumstances, no wonder the modest maiden would falter, and it would seem as if she was about to sink on the floor, when the rough, commanding voice of the auctioneer, would be heard, ringing out over the hum of voices.

"Walk pert now, as if you was going to church. Hold your head up. Let us see how spry you are. Notice that girl, gentlemen, if you please. See how she walks. There is the true Baltimore step—as fine a limbed girl, as you will ever see. Twelve hundred dollars bid!—who bids higher? A tidy girl; very smart; a good chambermaid and seamstress; seventeen years of age; raised in a genteel family—one of the first in Virginia; good size—beautiful form, as you see. Notice the girl, gentlemen. Here, Nina, step up once more. Twelve hundred fifty, I hear. Twelve—fifty! Twelve—fifty! Thirteen hundred—in time! Thank you, gentlemen. Going, for thirteen hundred."

And thus, for the second time, the bidding goes vigorously forward. As a final resort, and as if to excite the worst passions of the worst man, to become her purchaser, the auctioneer himself makes some indecent exposure of her person, accompanied with a fitting remark; and the bidding commences with new interest. Fifteen hundred dollars is reached, by this terrible process.

The auctioneer's hammer falls, and the fate of the poor girl is sealed. Another quickly ascends the platform, and a similar scene is enacted.

I stop not here to describe rows of beautiful boys, from twelve to fifteen years of age, dressed with the greatest regard to neatness and taste: blue pants, a roundabout jacket to match, with a clean collar turned over, *a la* Byron, fur hat, white stockings, and highly polished shoes, with their faces so intelligent, making a picture, when once seen never forgotten.

Instead, therefore, of its being impossible for masters to sell slaves, or in other words, "treat them as cattle," as Dr. Adams affirms, I found but one thing true in all the States, that if the master wished to sell them, it was a great advantage to him, to have them well dressed, and a point, they were not likely to neglect.

But this question of dress, has another aspect. To read Dr. A. one would suppose, that these fine clothes were all the gift of their masters, whereas, if he had made inquiries, he would have found, that the expense had been met, in half the instances, by the hard earnings of the poor slave, after his daily task for his master was accomplished.

It is very common at the South, for slaves to hire their time. They give their master as much as a common laborer can earn at the North. And no wonder that they delight to dress, since this is almost the only thing, in which they can resemble the white man. They have not the incentives to lay by money, that the whites have.

No wonder that they are pleased with gay colors, for in Africa, their native land, bird, beast and flower, all nature, is arrayed with the most gorgeous and brilliant colors.

The slaves, in favorable localities, have more opportunities for earning money to furnish themselves with necessaries and luxuries, than one would at first suppose. It is true of many, as one told me in the interior of Georgia, "If there is any money in the world, I must manage to have a part of it." Their masters encourage their industrious habits, by purchasing of them. A negro, that I met on the Alabama river, had raised one hundred turkies that year; these would probably net him, at least, one hundred dollars. In cities, where they hire their time, the industrious and hard working, especially, if they have a trade, are able to earn a handsome sum, over and above what they pay their masters.

The slaves, in the tobacco factories, become very dexterous, and earn great wages. One that I saw in St. Louis, was earning three dollars a day. The employers in Richmond, told me that their hands, would earn from three to eight dollars a week, for themselves, by overwork.

By some, it was spent in vice and dissipation, by others, in comforts for their families.

If he chooses to spend this all in dress, no wonder that he is able to make as respectable an appearance as Dr. Adams describes.

Or array a loved child with a, "white dress, profusely flounced, frilled ankles, light colored boots, mohair mitts and sunshade," &c.

Doing something for the body, while cruel laws forbid, that the mind of that child, should be expanded and adorned, with the gems of knowledge.

CHAPTER VI.

ARE THE SLAVES TREATED WITH CRUELTY?

THAT they are, is as strongly affirmed by abolitionists, as it is denied by the upholders of the system.

The question does not need any argument. Reason teaches, that four millions of human beings could not be held completely in the power, and at the will of others, without the infliction of scourgings, bonds, imprisonment, and often death. There is more or less of a tyrant's heart beating under the ribs of every man: and if irresponsible power is committed to men, there will be times, when they will use it as they ought not. Hence, no man should be allowed such power, but the rights of every one should be protected by law. Southern laws were made by the master for themselves, and not for the slave. And they deliver the one completely into the power of the other.

The exact amount of good or ill treatment can never be measured or ascertained. That there are cases of the most terrible severity, in moments of passion and otherwise, I have no doubt. And instances of great kindness, attachment, almost of parental affection, are equally true. Human nature is the same there as in other places. The justification or condemnation of the system, does not depend alone upon the treatment, be it good or bad. My experience among them led me to believe, that the slavehold[illegible] by birth, those brought up under the system, p[illegible] kinder masters than adopted citizens from Yankee land. And this opinion might be confirmed by any amount of testimony.

The negro usually dreads being thrown into the power of a northern master. And there are more of them held by northern capitalists, than one would have believed without examination.

There are, in that country, a great number of steam saw mills, owned and worked by northern men, with slave labor. And they make their boasts that "they whip them till their backs look like raw beef."

A true native born southerner is horrified at their cruelties.

An engineer in one of these mills, from Rhode Island, talked as coolly about giving one of the slaves under him, three hundred lashes, as of striking a dog that needed punishing. And then he had him chained to a heavy weight, before one of the furnaces, and kept him on duty, till he thought he was sufficiently subdued.

That negro, on a certain occasion, had once raised his hand to strike him, and the law in that State is that the hand must be cut off. But his master begged him off from that punishment; not from its inhumanity, but because it would ruin the negro. This engineer justified himself, from the fact, that when once employed in a cotton factory in Rhode Island, the stripes had been applied to his back, and he had worn them for weeks.

In the more northern Slave States, it is a standing threat to procure obedience, that "they will be sold to go South."

While, in the southern cities, slaves are sent by scores to the Calaboose to be whipped according to order.

In the Slave Market at Richmond, I asked a very fine looking slave that was about to be sold at auction, if I should purchase, and he should disobey me, what punishment I should inflict?

"Put me in your pocket, massa."

Do what? put you where? not understanding him.

"Sell me, massa."

That the whip is used freely, we infer from the fact, that in slave barracoons and auctions, they were always stripped to see in what condition the back might be.

Making some enquiries one day, of a negro in Georgia, on this point, he remarked,—"A heap of them have to be whipped. They won't mind their work—neglect it once, and if not whipped, think they can the second time. Massa must whip, else careless all the time." He had been whipped several times,—once for fighting with a negro. "He was not gwine to let any nigger impose on him," not he; too much spirit for that. He had been sold four times; three times to pay the debts of his master. A white man in the same State, of much experience, said, "There were but few but what had to be whipped."

One might pass much time at the South, and no cases of severe and cruel punishment, would come under his own eye. They would take some pains not to have a stranger witness any thing of the kind. But the incidental proof will continually occur, that such things are common.

Ascending the Alabama river on the steamer Coosa Belle, there was in our company, a planter from Texas, returning with his gang of negroes to North Carolina. Talking with some of the passengers of his bad luck, he incidently mentioned, that one very valuable slave of his, had been whipped to death that summer. Those with whom he was conversing, expressed no surprise, nor made any inquiries as to the circumstances. From their indifference, one might have inferred it was not a very uncommon occurrence.

But I had been brought up under other circumstances, and my curiosity was aroused to know something more of the facts. A very intelligent negro, who had been the play-mate of his master, had charge of the gang on the lower deck. I had previously made his acquaintance, and now went to him to ascertain the particulars. With deep emotion, he gave me the following facts:

Her name was Lucy; about sixteen years old; was not well, and could not accomplish her task; blood rushed to her head; could not see to do her work well; would stagger and fall.

The brutal and inhuman overseer, pretended she was "possuming," (feigning sickness,) had the lash applied to the poor girl's back, while prostrate on the ground, with his foot on her neck, slaves holding her extended limbs. When he had inflicted as much as he thought she could bear at once, she would be set at work.

By and by, the one that hired the slaves would appear in the field, and finding her lagging more than ever, would order a second infliction of the terrible lash. Poor Lucy's cries that they would have compassion on her, were heeded not, there was no eye to pity, or sympathize with that young girl in her physical weakness.

This treatment was continued, till she was so weak that her limbs refused to carry her to the field, and she was left in the negro quarters to die. My informant said she was a week dying—the most awful death he ever saw. In her friendless and sad condition, said he, I tried to tell her of heaven, and point her to Jesus, the sinner's friend. "But it 'peared like she could not sense any of these things, she had been so abused. I asked her one day to uncover her back, that I might see what condition it was in. There were great holes, an inch deep, where the flesh was rotted away, filled with worms. And the women that laid her out, after death, said, on her abdomen, was the print of the overseers's shoe, where he had kicked her, black and putrified, filled with worms."

Thus she died, and sleeps now in an unknown grave, in that land, to acquire which, that it might be cursed with Slavery, our nation poured out millions of gold, and sacrificed thousands of precious lives.

My informant told me of a man that died on the plantation that season, under the brutal treatment of the same overseer. They saw him punishing one, who did not return at night, to the quarters. The driver said, he had probably run into the woods. But, a few days after, they found him nearly rotton in the cornfield.

Probably, the incidental conversations that fall upon the ear of the traveler, between planters, negro drivers, and others, in bar-rooms, the saloons of steam boats, and public places generally, give one as truthful an idea of the horrors of the system, as can be obtained. In such places, among themselves, they talk as coolly about going out to hunt, and shoot run away negroes, as in other sections, about destroying wolves and bears. Certainly, the feelings of the community must have gone through a very hardning process, or the *burning of negroes alive*, would not be *such common occurrences*, as they are each year. A high degree of barbarism must exist in a community, to allow such a savage act of Indian cruelty to be perpetrated.

Again, it is evident that persons in the State Prisons of the South, are treated above par, have an easy, jovial time of it, or that slaves have severe treatment. For the officers of the Baton Rouge prison, assured me, "that no slave ought to be placed in them,—

that it was no punishment at all, they fared so much better than they did with their masters." And their general appearance, when contrasted with those on the outside, fully confirmed the truth of their assertion.

They did not seem to realize, how this fact gave the lie to their oft repeated assertion, "that the condition of the slave, was far to be preferred, to that of the Northern operative." We never heard it intimated at the North, that they would have their comforts increased, by partaking of State Prison fare.

Entering a house in New Orleans, to secure board, the door being ajar, and my knock not being heard, I passed to the parlor door, which was half open, and there the reason was obvious, why my call had not been answered. The mistress, a lady weighing a little less than two hundred, had backed one of her female servants into the corner of the room, was choking her with her left hand, and grasping at her protruding tongue with her right.

It was an instance of female garroting, which we think Northern ladies will be slow to adopt.

I started back, fearing lest I should be considered an intruder, upon a domestic scene, that was new to me. But she saw me, and releasing her hold, without any embarrassment on her part, bid me walk in, and be at home. Said she was only going to pull out the minxe's tongue, for talking about the boarders, "for you know," she says, "that many things occur in a boarding house, that must not be talked about." And that this is so, I suppose all who have had experience in such establishments, will admit. I took up my quarters with her, and found that she prided herself on being a model slaveholder. But from what I saw, day by day, I thought if hers' were treated in a model way, the others were surely to be pitied.

I was glad to find abundant evidence in the Southern States, that the treatment of the negroes is becoming more and more humane each year. They are being treated more and more like human beings. And this fact shows us the almost omnipotent power of public opinion, in the world, outside of the Slave States. And when, that hour comes, that we have no apologists for Slavery in the Free States, no divines preaching in cotton pulpits, or judges sitting, and pronouncing judgment on cotton cushions, Slavery will only be known as a matter of history.

CHAPTER VII.

IGNORANCE IN REGARD TO THE TREATMENT OF SLAVES.

ALL sorts of contradictory assertions are made by southern people, and persons who make a transient visit to some particular section, on this subject.

I was very much surprised, at the ignorance, of otherwise intelligent men, as to how negroes were treated, in neighborhoods, or States, even adjacent to that, where they were residing.

Different communities will have their own local laws, or customs on this subject. And one must visit all the States, to obtain the true bearings of this question.

One day, examining some very powerful whips, in a saddler's store, in Natches, a gentleman, who had made his fortune at the South, mistrusting, perhaps, the subject of my thoughts, he remarked, that overseers were not allowed to carry whips on plantations. That the planter would discharge him, unless he was able to govern without. But I seldom saw one, at his duty, but an efficient whip was his constant companion; and yet, there are plantations, where the whip is not carried to the field.

Others would tell me, "that husband and wife were seldom parted, that the slaves were well fed, not over-worked, &c., &c." I would tell them what I had seen, or ascertained, only one hundred miles from them.

"Well, it may be so *there*," they would say, "but in *this* region, it is so and so."

I asked but few slaves in the lower country, but they would tell me of a husband, or wife, or parents, that they had parted with, in the more northern slave States. Tens of thousands, on those cotton and sugar plantations, and among their house servants, have been brought from the slave breeding States farther north.

But there are kind masters, as well as severe,—persons that feel a certain degree of responsibility, to make, "their people," (as they call their slaves,) as comfortable as they can, under their circumstances.

There is one McGee, in Mississippi, that owns five hundred slaves. He builds a comfortable cabin for each couple, on their marriage, giving the husband a good broadcloth suit of clothes, and a corresponding bridal outfit to the lady. He provides for their moral instruction, by furnishing them a Pastor, at a salary of eight hundred dollars a year, besides his board, and the use of horses and carriages at his pleasure.

He treats his slaves so kindly, that none of them could be induced to leave him.

On a sugar plantation, that I visited in Louisiana, the slave women, if their rations were not sufficient, would go up to the, "Big House," and tell missus they were hungry, and were sure to be rewarded with something nice from her own stores.

Human nature is the same every where. At the North, we have some that treat those employed by them, with very little regard to their feelings, or rights, while others are thoughtful, considerate, and kind. But the employed here, can change employers at will, and in other ways, have their rights protected by law.

In regard to cruel treatment, it is enough to say, that all, North and South, have read Uncle Tom's Cabin. I found none to deny, that the terrible things there described, are true,—have their counterparts. Indeed, after her terrible, "Key," with names and dates, no sane man could deny it.

CHAPTER VIII.

THE INTERNAL SLAVE TRADE.

ONE of the sad sights which often meet the eye, reminding the stranger that he is in a foreign land, is the slave coffles, on their sad march from the blue hills and sunlit valleys of Virginia, Kentucky, and Tennessee, where they have spent their childhood, and leave parents and friends, for the dreaded plantations of those States, bordering on the Mexican Gulf. The practice of collecting droves of cattle, horses, and hogs, in the free States, for the great markets of Philadelphia, New York, and Boston, is just the counterpart of the collecting of these droves, of human cattle, for the great markets, in the South and South West. Speculators range the country, and where they find a man in debt, or an estate to be settled, they are on hand, to drive the best bargain they can.

And such has been the high price of cotton and sugar, for a few years past, that this trade, has now terrible activity.

By the common consent, of the civilized world, to engage in the foreign slave trade, is a crime worthy of death. But good christian men, may engage in the other, with no more compunctions of conscience, than in selling a yoke of oxen, or a pair of blood horses, to a drover.

Virginia—the mother of Presidents—is the greatest slave breeding State in the nation. There is no slave market in the country—and probably not in the world—where the business is carried on so briskly as in Richmond,—not thirty hours' ride from all the glorious free institutions of the land of the Puritans.* I was very much astonished, to find almost every other negro, that I questioned, in the south, to hail from Virginia.

Why was you sold? I would ask. "Massa was in debt—Massa wanted money—Massa died"—would be the invariable answer. I remember, one beautiful morning, in February—a tall, lank, tobacco chewing, planter, entered the cars, followed by a negro boy, hand cuffed, whom he seated nearly opposite me, himself taking a seat a little in advance. The boy was, apparently, about twenty, and as fine, intelligent, a looking negro, as could be found in a day's travel—would bring a thousand dollars, in any market. As the train moved on, his big eyes filled with tears. He gazed intently, upon each receding object, as if it was to be seen no more, and he would have it stereotyped upon his memory. I knew at once, that he was not thus manacled for crime. One would trust thousands, even life, to such an honest countenance.

Nevertheless, to ascertain the facts, I asked him, what he had been doing.

"Noting, massa." Where are you going? "'Spose to be sold—massa told me, he wanted me to go to —— village. It was to deceive me, and get me away quietly. For when we got to de village, he put dese irons on me, and he is gwine to sell me to get some

* Messrs. Dickinson, Hill & Co., negro auctioneers for Richmond, whose sales I attended daily, while in that city, report the amount of their business, during the year 'fifty six, as reaching the enormous sum of two millions. The sales by other firms, in that city, engaged in this terrible traffic, in human flesh, and the souls of men, would carry the sum total, over four millions of dollars.

money." As we neared, Richmond, and there was less danger, of his running away, the master took off his irons, that he might make, perhaps, a more respectable appearance.

When the speculator, has thoroughly ranged over a certain district, and collected a good assortment, for the Southern market, arrangements are made, for the long and weary journey, Southward. Mules and wagons, are purchased, to carry a tent, and things, necessary for the trip—food and cooking utensils,—also, for the children, and such as may become footsore by long travel. Where wood and water, may be obtained, they bivouac, for the night, sleeping in their covered wagons, and under a rudely pitched tent, or in the open air, around the blazing camp fire.

The light of another day, after a hastily prepared breakfast, finds them plodding, slowly, and wearily onward.

The journey accomplished, they may not be thrown immediately into the market, especially if they have lost flesh by the way. But, are well fed, washed, hair trimmed, new clothed, and great pains taken, by making them as tidy as possible, to put them into saleable order.

The collectors, of Southern statistics, those best acquainted with this subject, estimate that one hundred thousand, are taken yearly, from the northern slave breeding states, to those further South.

Families grow rich, by slave breeding, in this christian land—horrible as it may seem—the same as the farmers of the Free States, by raising stock.

One man was pointed out to me, who began with a small capital, in this way, and was then worth twenty thousand dollars. But who shall estimate the tears, or the amount of sorrow, of broken hearts and disappointed hopes, caused by this terrible conscription, of one hundred thousand, of the young, driven to that region, which, in one sense, is like the grave, for, from it, there is no return.

How many a Virginian mother, with her crushed and bleeding heart, can claim as but too true, in regard to her daughters, sold into Southern bondage, the words of Whittier:—

"Gone! gone!—sold and gone,
To the rice swamp dank and lone;
Where the slave whip ceaseless swings,
Where the noisome insect stings,
Where the fever demon strews
Poison with the falling dews,
Where the sickly sunbeams glare
Through the hot and misty air,

Gone! gone!—sold and gone,
To the rice swamps dank and lone,
From Virginia's hills and waters,—
Wo is me, my stolen daughters!

Gone! gone!—sold and gone,
To the rice swamp dank and lone.
There no mother's eye is near them,
There no mother's ear can hear them,
Never, when the torturing lash
Seams their back with many a gash,
Shall a mother's kindness bless them,
Or a mother's arms caress them.

Gone! gone!—&c.

Gone! gone!—sold and gone,
To the rice swamp dank and lone.
O! when weary, sad and slow,
From the fields at night they go,
Faint with toil, and racked with pain,
To their cheerless homes again,—
There no brother's voice shall greet them,
There no father's welcome meet them.

Gone! gone!—&c.

Gone! gone!—sold and gone,
To the rice swamp dank and lone.

From the tree whose shadow lay
On their childhood's place of play;
From the cool spring where they drank;
Rock, and hill, and rivulet bank;
From the solemn house of prayer,
And the holy councils there,—

Gone! gone!—&c.

Gone! gone!—sold and gone,
To the rice swamp dank and lone;
Toiling through the weary day,
And at night the spoiler's prey.
O! that they had earlier died,
Sleeping calmly, side by side,
Where the tyrant's power is o'er,
And the fetter galls no more!

Gone! gone!—&c.

Gone! gone!—sold and gone,
To the rice swamp dank and lone.
By the holy love He beareth,
By the bruised reed He spareth,
O, may He, to whom alone
All their cruel wrongs are known,
Still their hope and refuge prove,
With a more than mother's love!

Gone! gone!"—&c.

But an element, of this internal Slave Trade, more sad and sickening to our common humanity, than any thing else, is the astounding fact, that fathers, not unfrequently, sell *their own children,* or leave them to be sold by others, and continued in slavery, after the death of the father and master.

No one need travel far at the South, without obtaining such abundant proof on this point, as to feel there is no lower depth, to which a man may sink himself.

One would naturally suppose, that the least reparation would be, to emancipate both mother and child.

Passing through Georgia—not far from Flat Shoals

Factory—I was pointed to a place, by the side of the road, where one of these droves from Virginia, had been encamped for some weeks.

One of their number, a young lady of about eighteen years, was not in a condition to travel; and the speculator was very anxious to sell her, that he might not be detained with the others. My informant said, "she was the handsomest woman he ever saw. Not a mark of negro blood about her. Planters came, and looked at her, but were unwilling to purchase, she was *so white.*

One said, "he would not have her for any price—that she was a heap handsomer than his wife."

The other negroes paid her the greatest defference, and waited on her, in the most attentive manner.

As soon after the birth of the child, (which all said, was the very picture of the owner of the lady), as the mother was able to travel, the drove commenced its weary line of march towards a market, where the father doubtless found, that the fair complexion of the mother, enhanced her value, instead of diminishing it.

The sale of one, not as young, as the last mentioned, but which had been allowed to grow up, under the eye of the father, and ought to have found a high place, in his heart's best and warmest affections, is thus described, by another of New England's poets:

THE QUADROON GIRL.

The slaver in the broad lagoon,
  Lay moored with idle sail;
He waited for the rising moon
  And for the evening gale.

Under the shore his boat was tied,
  And all her listless crew
Watched the grey alligator slide,
  Into the still Bayou.

Odors of orange flowers and spice,
  Reached them from time to time,
Like airs that breathe from Paradise
  Upon a world of crime.

The planter, under his roof of thatch,
  Smoked thoughtfully and slow;
The slaver's thumb was on the latch,
  He seemed in haste to go.

He said—"My ship at anchor rides
  In yonder broad lagoon;
I only wait the evening tides
  And rising of the moon."

Before them, with her face upraised,
  In timid attitude,
Like one half curious, half amazed,
  A Quadroon maiden stood.

Her eyes were large, and full of light,
  Her arms and neck were bare;
No garment she wore, save a kirtle bright
  And her own long, raven hair.

And on her lips there played a smile,
  As holy, meek, and faint,
As lights in some cathedral aisle
  The features of a saint.

"The soil is barren, the farm is old,"
  The thoughtful Planter said;
Then looked upon the slaver's gold,
  And then upon the maid.

His heart within him was at strife
  With such accursed gains;
For he knew whose passions gave her life,
  Whose blood ran in her veins.

But the voice of nature was too weak;
  He took the glittering gold!
Then pale as death grew the maiden's cheek,
  Her hands as icy cold.

The slaver led her from the door,
  He led her by the hand,
To be his slave and paramour,
  In a strange and distant land!

CHAPTER IX.

DO THE SLAVES DESIRE LIBERTY?

"Ask not the shepherd boy, who, 'neath the hedge,
Sits linking cherry stones, how fair is freedom—
He was *always* free."

WE were constantly told that they did not. That they would not take it, if offered. "That a *happier, better used,* or *more contented* set of operatives could not be found." Indeed, the owners ever affirmed, to me, that the *care*, the *anxiety*, the *real toil* was theirs. While the negro had only to sing, rejoice, and drive dull care away." Knowing that food, shelter, and a home, were secured to him, as long as he should live. To hear them talk, one was led to wonder, why they did not propose to change places with the negro.

They would point, in confirmation, to some, that had been offered their liberty, and would not accept it; to others, who had been North, and voluntarily returned.

Said a lady, in Savannah, to me, "Ask any of these servants, if they will leave me, and go North with you, and be free?"

Their happy, well fed, contented condition, has been, "the harp of a thousand strings," upon which the Southern press, has played innumerable changes, for years past.

Still we ask the question, Do the Slaves desire Freedom?

You might as well, ask the herds of wild buffalo

and horses, that roam at will, over the flower gemmed savannahs of the West and South, whose tread, when aroused, is like the shock of an earthquake, whether they would love the yoke and the harness, better than their liberty, and the freedom of the plain, which is now their birthright.

Could they understand its import, the scorn they would visit on the presumptuous questioner, would be more than his life would be worth.

If the slave is happy and contented, as we are so often told, what means that cry of insurrection—rebellion, which echoes forth from Maryland to Texas? Why is each white man armed to the teeth, and fear drive quiet sleep from the eyes, and blanch every countenance? Why are some whipped to death, and others hung? Why should the, "Clarksville Jeffersonian" use the following language, which is but a sample of other papers:—

"Fearful and terrible examples should be made, and, if need be, the faggot and the flame should be brought into requisition, to show these deluded maniacs, the fierceness, vigor, the swiftness and completeness, of the white man's vengeance. Let a terrible example be made in every neighborhood, when the crime can be established; and, if necesssary, let every tree in the country bend with negro meat. *We must strike terror*, and make a lasting impression, for only in such a course, can we find guaranties of future security."

While visions of burning dwellings, and slaughtered citizens, keep them in constant fear and anxiety, the Free State manufacturer sleeps in the greatest quietness, without weapons, and with no need of locks or bolts, in the midst of his operatives, who, if we were to believe the South, are far worse treated, than the slaves among them. Rebellion is only to be feared, where there are *wrongs* to be redressed, and *rights* to be recovered.

There is *cause*, why those masters should fear, and will ever be, as long as slavery exists.

A slave in New Orleans wished me to buy him, and let him work out his freedom, said he would work his fingers off for that purpose. I told him the white folks affirmed, the slaves did not wish for liberty.

"Hi!" he exclaimed, with a broad grin; "not wish for liberty? *Let them try us!* Beast free; bird free; fish free; everything want to be free. It is kind of natural. Not wish to be free!" he repeated, and laughed heartily, as though it was the best joke of the season.

And, in substance, I received but that one answer, as often as I proposed the question.

And yet, it is true, that there are cases of favorite servants, that for various reasons, would not accept of liberty, precious as is the boon, if they must break up all their associations there, and go North, to enjoy it. Just as we have thousands in our cities, and manufacturing villages, struggling to keep themselves from starvation, when, by going west, and taking up government land, they might soon be in independent circumstances.

The following dialogue, which Mr. F. A. Olmstead, had in Louisiana, with a very intelligent, Virginia born negro, both illustrates the desire of the negroes, for liberty, and how groundless is the argument, so much in vogue at the South, that the negroes would not work, if the fear of the lash was removed, in other words, if they were free.

William, the slave in question, acknowledged he had one of the kindest masters in all that region.

OLMSTEAD. Well, now. wouldn't you rather live on such a plantation, than to be free?"

WILLIAM. Oh, no, sir; I'd rather be free! Oh,

yes, sir, I'd like it better to be free; I would dat, master.

OLMS. Why would you?

WIL. Why, you see, master, if I was free—if I was *free*, I'd have *all* my time to myself. I'd rather work for myself—I'd like dat better.

OLMS. But then, you know, you'd have to take care of yourself, and you'd get poor.

WIL. No, sir, I would not get poor, I would get rich; for you see, master, then I'd work *all de time* for myself.

OLMS. Suppose all the black people on your plantation, or all the black people in the country were made free, at once, what do you think would become of them? What would they do? You do not suppose there would be much sugar raised, do you?

WIL. Why, yes, master, I do. Why not, sir? What *would* de brack people do? Wouldn't dey hab to work for dar libben? And de wite people own all de land—war dey goin' to work? Dey hire demself right out again, and work all de same as before. And den, wen dey work for demself, dey work *harder* dan dey do now, to get more wages—a heap harder. I tink so, sir. I would do so, sir. I would work for hire. I don't own any land—I hab to wòrk right away again, for massa, to get some money.

OLMS. The black people talk among themselves, about this, do they; and they think so, generally?

WIL. Oh, yes, sir; dey talk so; dats wat dey tink.

OLMS. Then they talk about being *free* a good deal, do they?

WIL. Yes, sir; dey—dat is, dey say, dey wish it was so; dat is all dey talk, master—dat's all, sir.

His caution being evidently excited, Mr. O. changed the subject.

CHAPTER X.

ESCAPE OF SLAVES.

THESE are are continually occurring, though surrounded with such tremendous difficulties, and the penalty so fearful, if they do not succeed. Over fifty thousand dollars worth of this kind of property, escaped from the vicinity of Norfolk, Va., during the year 'fifty five, as I heard a gentleman affirm, in the Virginia House of Delegates.

They were engaged in passing that iniquitous law, by which any Yankee vessel, that visits their waters, must be searched, and then the Yankee skipper, must pay five dollars, to the officer that does it.

This ought to be the last ounce, that breaks the camel's back. For it is suffering ourselves to be *whipped* or *skinned* alive, and then meekly bowing the knee, and paying a man five dollars, for doing it.

I do not wonder the whole South, calls us, "A miserable, money loving race. That, with hat under arm, would most obsequiously bow, and kiss the great toe of any slave holder, if we could only make five cents by it."

They used to throw this in my face every where. *And I knew it was but two true, of many.*

A lady living near Nashville, had a servant boy, whose mother was dead, to which, for various reasons, she was very much attached.

She dressed him like a gentleman, made him her favorite house servant. When fully grown, she hired him as a kind of porter and clerk, to a merchant, in Nashville. In one of his visits home, he requested her to sell him. She was startled, asked, "Why? Have I not always treated you well? Dressed you in fine style? Done every thing for you that you needed? &c." "Yes! missus. All *very true,* no fault to find. *But I may die.* Life is very uncertain. And you cannot so well afford to loose me, as the man I work for.

But she was willing to risk that contingency, and replied, "No, James, you are too good a servant, I can 't think of selling you." At the proper time, he left her, to return to his employer, as she supposed. By and by, a letter came, asking why James did not return. She thought he had already been there weeks.

The sequel proved, that he had turned his course towards the north star. After a while, a letter came from Canada, stating that he had tasted of liberty, and that it was so sweet, he wanted still to enjoy it. And would remit her the price of himself, as soon as he could acquire it. But she was in easy circumstances, and was so attached to him, that the money was nothing, she was willing to give him his freedom, under the circumstances.

Another case, that occurred in Alabama. A negro used to ride to school, with his young master, as a kind of waiter, and for company, through the woods. As he heard them recite, he would remember it, and in regard to many of the branches, it was the same as if he recited. He became quite a scholar, and delighted in reading.

And it was no uncommon occurrence, for him to be seen reading the papers, on one side of the lamp, and his master doing the same on the other. By and by, he took a horse and provisions, and put for the Free States. Gained them, and wrote back to his master, that he would send him the price for himself, as soon as he was able to earn it.

But in this, as in the other case, the owner did not lay it very much to heart.

There are more, or less cases, where they do not take much pains, to recover them. And then a multitude of others, when they would feign move heaven and earth, to accomplish it. They must have them, *dead* or *alive*.

Just before I arrived in Jacksonville, Florida, a slave escaped, in a lumber vessel, North. His master followed him to Baltimore, and if he had been two hours sooner, would have secured him. A fine negro, worth one thousand dollars, in that market.

Two others came very near escaping ; were betrayed, by one of their own color. They were punished awfully. Thirty nine lashes, for nine days in succession, till their backs were like raw beef.

The very intelligent slave, that gave me the information, said, " that the fear of such terrible punishment, was all that kept him from making the attempt, to gain his freedom. He gave his master, a dollar a day for his time, and boarded and clothed himself, had what he could make over.

This, certainly, was pretty good interest, that the master was receiving, on one thousand or fifteen hundred dollars.

They will not give up a system readily, when they can make such profits. This slave said, he meant to so live, as to get safely through this wicked world, and secure a home in heaven, where he could be *free*.

And he had my best wishes, that such might be the case.

Those acquainted with the physical geography of the South, are aware, that it abounds with interminable swamps, impenetrable cane brakes, and inaccessible everglades. The safe and secure hiding place, for Indians, run away slaves; also, being the natural home, the paradise of bears, wolves, alligators, and snakes of enormous size, as well as most virulent poison. Here are thousands of acres, the soil composed of decayed vegetable matter, saturated with water, and one vast quagmire, shaking for roods around to the tread of man. Besides those mighty monarchs of the forest—which the rich soil, the warm climate, and abundant moisture, so naturally produce—there is a most luxurious growth of canes, shrubs, vines, creepers, briars, in short, every thing, that heat, richness, and moisture, can produce—forming a dense brake or jungle. A person might pass within a rod of another, and not see him. It would take a man, hours, with a sharp cane knife, to work his way a few rods. It was to such a hiding place, that "Dred," betook himself with his companions in tribulation.

If there are few that possess his character, nevertheless, there are many that dwell in such wild homes.

Here and there may be an acre or two, a kind of island, raised two or three feet above the surrounding swamp—where they build their cabins, and plant their corn.

The creeks, or sluices winding through that tangled sea of green abound with fish. If one wished for a quiet sylvan retreat, away from the noise and turmoil of life, where they might be in communion with nature only, it is here. "Where evergreen trees, mingling freely with the deciduous children of the forest, form dense jungles, verdant all the year round, and which afford shelter to numberless birds, with whose warbling the leafy desolation perpetually resounds. Climbing vines, and parasitic plants, of untold splendor and boundless exhuberance of growth, twine, and interlace, and hang, from the heights of the highest trees, pennons of gold and purple, triumphant banners, which attest the solitary majesty of nature.

A species of parasitic moss wreaths its abundant draperies from tree to tree, and hangs in pearly festoons, through which show the scarlet berry and green leaves of the American holly." The cold and barren North, where the ice king reigns for half the year, can furnish nothing like this feature of the Southern landscape.

The poor slave, when his patience is clear exhausted, and madened beyond endurance at the hardships of his lot, betakes himself to these impenetrable fastnesses, to associate with wild beasts less savage than man.

Then it is that,

> Away to the dismal swamp he speeds,
>   His path was rugged and sore,
> Through tangled juniper, beds of reeds,
> Through many a fen, where the serpent feeds,
>   And man never trod before.
>
> And, when on the earth he sunk to sleep,
>   If slumber his eyelids knew,
> He lay where the deadly vine doth weep
> Its venemous tears, that nightly steep
>   The flesh with blistering dew.

Nor can they well be secured, without those terrible blood hounds, from whom there is no escape, except the slave is able to swim, and there is a stream of water, into which he may plunge, and foil them. Those dogs are so well trained, that you have only to let them smell of an axe helve, or hoe handle, that the slave has been using, and they will get on his trail, and are almost sure to find him. Like Davy Crocket's coon, the poor negro might as well give up at once.

From those swamps, they issue out at night, and

forage for provision, in the best way they can. The slaves always divide their scanty supplies with them. They become expert in trapping wild animals, and eke out a precarious existence year after year. Prefering such a wild life of freedom, to the merciless crack of the slave driver's whip, over their backs. They, in different ways, not unfrequently, manage to obtain fire arms and ammunition, which places them in quite independent circumstances. The owner often knows that the runaway, is in such a swamp or woods. The same as when, in a new country, a man's stock strays away.

He knows where it is, although he is not able to secure it.

In such a case, he often sells the title to it, "Running." And the buyer takes the risk, of securing the property. If secured, he is put into the slave coffle, and marched South. And sold without any very strong recommend of character, at the buyer's risk.

On a sugar plantation, in Louisiana, I saw one such slave, that had been in the woods a year; had voluntarily surrendered himself. He ran away, because he, with other slaves of the plantation, were to be sold, while his wife—belonging to another man—would be left behind.

When he found that the running title had been bought, by a man, that he liked, he willingly came, and gave up his lonely, unsocial life.

But he had been so long without work, and so exposed, that he had almost lost the use of his hands, and in other respects, was disabled. The master, told the overseer, not to give him hard tasks, till he was limbered up.

Slaves are often hired out by their owners, to some one that needs their labor, but has not capital to buy, or, for other reasons, does not care to.

In such cases, if they are sick, or run away, the one that hires must suffer the loss. And this class, if they do not like their employer, are very apt to betake themselves to the woods; returning at the end of the year, to their old master, to be hired to some other person, that they may like better. He rejoicing so much, that they did not betake themselves to a free State, that they escape all punishment.

Those tangled thickets, Dismal Swamps, and reedy fens, the homes of the runaway negroes, if it is right to apply a word, so full of tender associations, to their wild haunts, have been thus graphically described by the pen of Longfellow:

"In the dark fens of the Dismal Swamp,
The hunted negro lay;
He saw the fire of the midnight camp,
And heard at times the horse's tramp,
And a bloodhound's distant bay.

Where will-o'-the-wisp and glow worms shine,
In bulrush and in brake;
Where waving mosses shroud the pine,
And the cedar grows, and the poisonous vine
Is spotted like the snake;

Where hardly a human foot could pass,
Or a human heart would dare,—
On the quaking turf of the green morass,
He crouched in the rank and tangled grass,
Like a wild beast in his lair.

A poor old slave! infirm and lame,
Great scars deformed his face;
On his forehead he bore the brand of shame,
And the rags that hid his mangled frame,
Were the livery of disgrace.

All things above were bright and fair,
All things were glad and free;
Lithe squirrels darted here and there,
And wild birds filled the echoing air,
With songs of liberty!

On him alone was the doom of pain,
From the morning of his birth;
On him alone the curse of Cain,
Fell like the flail on the garnered grain,
And struck him to the earth."

CHAPTER XI.

COLORED PEOPLE SLAVEHOLDERS.

I was not prepared to find this true, to so large an extent as it is. Even persons holding them, who have themselves tasted the sweets of Slavery. The laws against emancipation, are not so strict in Alabama, and Louisiana, and some of the States bordering on the gulf of Mexico, as in those farther North. Cases of emancipation of favorite slaves, are not unfrequent. Others, of enterprising habits, are allowed to purchase their freedom.

Perhaps the master, owes his life, or that of a loved wife, or child, in an attack of Yellow Fever, to the careful nursing of a servant, who risked her own life, to save that of her master.

In that fearful hour, when the dark wing of the pestilence was hovering over them, that servant was worth her weight in gold. Money could not have purchased such services. While under the exercise of this feeling of gratitude, he executes a deed of emancipation, and that chattel, goes through the wondrous transformation, of becoming a man, or woman, as the case may be.

In other instances, the woman, may have sustained that peculiar relation to the master, which led him, at his death, or before, to give her, or her children, or both, free papers.

From various causes, take the whole State, through, such free persons are found. And they, are more likely to acquire property, than those colored persons born free.

There is a Mrs. Pope, in Mobile, whose master freed her when she was twenty-five. She was a lady of enterprise,—opened a fashionable boarding house, nursed northern folks, that were sick, and in different ways, made money rapidly, till now she is worth fifty thousand dollars, or more,—owns some twenty slave girls,—hires out those she does not need, in her own establishment.

They must all bring her six bits at night, or a tremendous thrashing awaits them. Her daughters have been well educated,—play beautifully on the harp and piano. Are fashionably dressed, and make as fine an appearance, as any that walk the streets of that city. One of her daughters married a white man, and they reside in New Orleans. All gave her the character, of being a very hard mistress.

In Louisana, it is not at all uncommon for colored men to own slaves, and work sugar plantations.

Visiting the celebrated battle ground, below New Orleans, I entered a sugar house, near, and, in a very interesting conversation with a French sugar maker, who, was entirely opposed to Slavery, I asked him how the white folks liked to have the colored people become the owners of slaves and plantations.

"Oh!" he replied, "dey likes it first rate; it satisfies dare conscience. If de black man can enslave his own color, when he has de power, his own bredren, den we are fully justified to enslave them too."

Some of these rich, free colored persons, go to France, or some part of the continent, marry a white woman, return with her; and it is not uncommon, for a pretty white woman, to be seen carrying a very black baby through the street, or dandling it on her knees at home.

These colored slaveholders, of whom I am speaking, are of mixed blood, and the majority of them, the descendants of the French and Spanish planters, and their Slaves.

There is, of course, every variety of color among them. When the State was annexed, they came in as free citizens. Many of them are well educated, and if you have occasion to call at their houses, you will be received in a gentlemanly manner, and find them living in the same style, as white people under similar circumstances.

They will converse with you in French or English, as occasion may require. In this class, are to be seen, the most beautiful ladies in the world, probably. A dash of blood from so many different nations, in that genial clime, has produced a style of beauty, that must be seen, in order to be appreciated.

In one Parish, in the last Presidential election, over fifty votes were cast by these colored slaveholders.

From what I was able to learn, I am inclined to think, there is no State in the Union, where the rights of all classes of persons, are better protected by law, than in Louisiana, or where the colored man is more respected.

A nearly full blooded negro, owning one hundred slaves, has the most tastefully ornamented grounds, and neatest cottage, that can be found in riding many hundred miles:—is well educated, and keeps a private tutor for his children.

CHAPTER XII.

DOES THE SOUTH INTEND TO DIVIDE THE UNION, UNLESS WE LET THEM GOVERN US, AND HAVE EVERY THING THEIR OWN WAY, IN YEARS TO COME, AS THEY HAVE DONE IN YEARS PAST? OR IS IT MERE THREATS, BRAGGADOCIO—AN ATTEMPT TO AWE THE NORTH, AND INSPIRE FEAR?

I FULLY believe, they intend to do what they say. It is, with them, "fifty-four—forty," or fight. There will be no backing down, on their part. It is not reasonable, to suppose, that those, who rule with such iron sway at home—whose word is law, and who have always had what they demanded, will quietly yield to those claims of *equal rights*, which the giant North thinks she has a right to demand. Then they are entirely ignorant of our *strength*, *wealth*, and *energy*. They think the Free States are entirely dependent on them, and that we could scarcely exist a day, should they step out of the Union; that they have only to raise the flag of a Southern Confederacy, and the whole North, with tears, would be on their knees, at the slaveholders' feet, beseeching them not to bring swift and entire destruction, on the East, North and West. Perhaps nothing astonished me more, than their ignorance of Northern resources. They used to entreat me, with the greatest earnestness, to make known fully to the North, that for *our own sakes*, unless we silenced our presses, and ceased talking about the rights of the "Niggers," they would step out of the Union—have nothing more to do with such villains; while we, on our part, from that moment, would have nothing to

do, but to die, and obtain as decent a burial as possible.

I used to tell them, that whether it was life or death to us, they might as well think of stopping the sun from rising on the morrow, or gravitation from exerting its power, as to suppose that this discussion will cease, till every slave has the rights, which God has given to every human being.

From free and familiar conversation, on this point, in all the States, I am fully convinced they all have the feeling of Mrs. S——, a very intelligent widow lady, of East Florida, a Methodist, who told me, "If she had fifty sons, she would send them all forth to fight for slavery; and, old as she was, she was ready to go herself."

Here was the true Southern spirit, cropping out—in a lady, nearer sixty, than fifty, if I might be allowed to, "guess."

Here is an extract, from the teachings of the Southern press, upon this point. And one must be very ignorant of Southern character, and of the warmth of Southern blood, to suppose that such appeals can be made to their prejudices, their pride, their self interest, and not result in their drawing the sword:—

"Will you submit to the oppression of the North? To have your rights of private property violated *by your creature*, Congress? Will you submit to have yourselves and your children placed on terms of equality with the Negro race? Are you willing to leave your children to the curse of a hostile, freed negro population! Will you submit to be made an inferior, degraded caste in the Federal Union, with Northern *and Negro* masters?

"Are you willing to witness a scene of perpetual and cruel war of races, that would make your country a spectacle of horror, desolation, and bloodshed? Are we so in love with that *Union*, with our Northern masters, as to be willing to sacrifice our dearest interests rather than sever it? Are we willing to give up all, suffer all, sacrifice all? Is this the spirit of Southern patriotism? Is this the end of Southern chivalry? Will the fiery spirit of the South thus cower under injustice and oppression? If so, they are 'cowards—craven, and crouching,' and are worthy of no better fate! Will the Southern people submit to the operation of a law excluding them, with their property, from that territory which they helped to purchase and win; for which they sent their children out to battle? If so, they have yielded the whole question, and emancipation becomes then inevitably certain; and its accomplishment is only a question of expediency as to time.

"*One inch of ground yielded, one principle given up, one outpost abandoned*, and we are crushed; Southern safety and Southern prosperity are forever doomed! Will you fold your hands to slumber? Will you sit still until the day of danger *comes?* Then Sampson is shorn of his locks, and the day of his humiliation is at hand. Nothing but an effort. speedy, earnest, general, and powerful, can save the South from a moral subjugation, and from miseries against which it is the duty of wisdom and patriotism to provide."

Such is the language of the Southern papers, and as far as read, will have effect.

But as we understand the subject, their doom is sealed. They have awoke too late, to the peril of their situation. They have no men to spare, to march to the, "Border," and defend their rights, as the writer we have quoted, in one place, advises. All that own slaves, will be needed at home, to guard that servile population, that chafe so terribly under their bonds.

Nevertheless, they have such extravagant views of their own strength, and of the cowardice and weakness of the Free States, that they will most assuredly draw the sword, in defence of the right to enslave men, and then, just as certainly, *perish in the struggle.*

We may be mistaken, in our opinion; but with all the light we have been able to obtain, such a result, seems to us, certain.

In their houses, are found plenty of books, demonstrating, (to them) that the Bible endorses the "Peculiar Institution." While ethics, metaphysics, law, jurisprudence, and political economy, are all warped, welted, twisted and moulded to form buttresses and supports for the system.

"If the North and the South ever do lock horns, and push for it, there is no doubt which goes into the ditch. One weighs seventeen millions, the other eleven millions; but, besides, the southern animal is exceedingly weak in the whole hind quarters, four millions in weight, not strong in the fore quarters of the same bulk; and stiff only in the neck and head; while the Northern Creature is weak only in the neck and horns, which would become stiff enough in a little time."

CHAPTER XIII.

A DIFFERENCE, WHICH THE SOUTH, AND NEHEMIAH ADAMS, D. D., OF THE NORTH, DO NOT SEEM TO BE ABLE TO APPRECIATE.

In all parts of the South, we were continually reminded of evils which exist, in the social condition of thousands, among the operatives in the Free States, and told that when we had ameliorated their situation, and raised them in the scale of humanity, it would be time to sympathize with, and talk about the suffering in the Slave States. But so long as we have a vicious and ignorant population, both white and black, in the great centres of our population, it is down-right impertinence, to mention any evils which exist among them. The wonder is, that a man of Doctor Adam's intelligence, could not see through such sophistry, and should ever have penned the following sentence, speaking of certain emigrants from Great Britain and Ireland:—

"Human nature, in civilized life, seldom goes down to worse degradation than in them, and the land that suffers such specimens of moral deformity to go from her, not in solitary instances, but in ship loads, never should offer *compassionating prayers* and *exhortations*, much less reproaches, with regard to any other nation, until this class of her own subjects is improved." He ridicules the idea of English ladies, in their large hearted christian sympathy, showing any feeling of pity, or commiseration for those of their own sex, suffering undescribable indignities and wrongs, in the legalized markets of American licentiousness, till every evil and occasion of suffering has been removed at home.

The Rev. Doctor, as well as the slaveholder, seem to ignore the fact, that the evils, the sorrows, and sufferings of Slavery, are the *legitimate results of the institution, its invariable attendant*, sustained and legalized by *law*; while the ignorance, vice, and consequent suffering in the free cities of the North, are incidental to man's free agency, exists, contrary to law, and in spite of all the efforts, which noble hearted men and women, by night and day, are putting forth to remove them. Those Philanthropists, whom the Doctor would cover with obloquy, for their efforts to alleviate the sufferings in Slave land, are the very ones that are doing the most at home. Wherever rum is sold freely, there will always be untold suffering. But let a, "Maine Law," be sustained, and those leprous spots of our great cities, would only be known as a matter of history.

Besides, *we acknowledge these evils and bewail them.*

We open our churches, and light up our splendid halls, and crowd them with an intelligent audience, to listen to any one, who may have a good word to offer, as to the removal of any evil that exists among us. But the South unblushingly deny, that any such evils as are charged, exist among them. They affirm that theirs is the natural, Paradisean state of society, and they show a guilty conscience, in that they will allow no man, on their own soil, to speak publicly of the evils of Slavery. It is too late in the day for them to say, that all outside of Slave territory, have no interest in this question.

The common brotherhood of man, is beginning to be acknowledged, and in whatever part of the world, one is being wronged by another, every other human being, though separated by the diameter of the earth, has a right to rebuke the oppressor, and say, "hands off, that suffering one is my brother, or sister."

Should we ever *legalize* the evils of the North, deny their existence, treat a man to a coat of tar and feathers, who should dare to allude to them; then would the taunts and the jeers, of the South, and Doctor A., and the emphatic, "look at home," have some point and edge, and be in not so bad taste.

Certainly, the love of man to his brother, human benefactions and sympathies, do not so abound, that there need be a word said to restrain their flow, either Northward or Southward, or from those in the old world, to us in the new. Let them flow far and wide, for there is no danger that the earth will be too soon relieved of her weight of woe and sorrow.

CHAPTER XIV.

BABY HOUSES.

On all the large and well conducted cotton, rice, and sugar plantations, of the South, there is what is called a, " Baby House."

This is the only labor-saving institution, that we remember to have met with. Not very much to be commended for its humanity; but is in keeping with the rest of the slave system. As soon after the birth of the child as possible, the mother must take her place in the field, and perform her allotted task. While all the children, from a few days, to four or five years old, are gathered into one cabin, and are placed under the care of some of the grandmothers, disabled or superanuated negresses, who are not able to work in the field. I always visited these baby houses, with a great deal of interest. For what on earth is a more pleasant sight, than these buds of living beauty, scattered around our pathway, fresh from the gardens of Paradise?

If some enterprising Barnum could send to the North, one of these, " baby houses," with its various colored inmates, and all its fixtures, without the slightest change, his fortune would be made.

Mothers of the, " upper ten," in New York, Boston, and other cities in the Free States, whose children must be rocked to sleep, in cradles of the costliest construction, would be not a little surprised, at the rude structures, in which these children, obtain so much quiet sleep. Instead of crying to have some one take them up, cuddle, carry, or amuse them in some way, which would be utterly impossible, so few are the nurses, these children learn to amuse themselves, and that the exercise of the lungs in crying, injures no one, but itself. The older children, are fed with porridge, boiled rice, or mush and syrup, from the sugar house. While, the mothers of the nursing ones, are allowed to return to the cabin in the middle of the forenoon and afternoon, to attend to their maternal duties. Or, perhaps, at eleven o'clock, and stay till one, P. M.,—leaving the field at night an hour or two before the others, or, whenever they have completed their tasks.

Custom, in different States and plantations, varies in this respect.

While I was on one plantation, the mothers were engaged in, "Shucking corn," near the, "baby house," and were kept under lock and key, during the hours of labor, lest the mother, hearing the cry of her darling for that food, which she alone could impart, would have her maternal feelings, so excited, that she would rush to press her babe to her bosom.

Northern mothers, who are so ready to listen to, and answer the child's first cry of distress, will think that this feature of Slavery cannot be too strongly condemned.

There was, in this last mentioned, "baby house," a child of one of the favorite servants, at the, "Big House," as white, and beautiful, as any that were found in Barnum's great baby show. Yet it must take its chance, with the rest on the plantation, though not so highly favored in parentage and color. It seemed like a white rose bud, or lily of the valley, strangely out of place.

As I bent over it, as it lay sweetly sleeping, smiling, and dreaming of heaven, I could but think of its sad future, unless God, in mercy, should early transplant it to the gardens of Paradise.

Thus, being allowed so little pleasure in the society

of her children, is it to be wondered at, that the slave mother's heart is so filled with sadness? And the feelings of thousands, was doubtless expressed, in the language of one, who said to me, "it is a heap of trouble for slaves to raise children. It don't pay, case not *ours*—dey belongs to massa; and when dey gets big, massa sells them, and gets a heap of money. De pain, de sorrow, de trouble, belong to us, not de chil'ern, to comfort us in old age."

CHAPTER XV.

BEDS FOR THE NEGROES.

THE whites, evidently, consider that it is, "of no account," to provide such luxuries for them. It is taken for granted, that they can sleep at any time, in any place, in any way, if they have a blanket, or rug to wrap around them.

House servants, as far as I observed, drop down anywhere to sleep, if it is only in a place convenient to be called. Beds for the plantation negroes, were of the rudest, and hardest kinds.

The tyllindria, or moss, which we consider so valuable for beds, grows, in those lower States, in the greatest profusion. The trees almost bend with it. Yet the negroes are too indifferent to gather it for their own convenience, though they bring it, in abundance, to the market for sale.

Servants, traveling with their masters, on steamboats, must sleep where they can. One instance, which met my notice, seemed hard. Passing from Florida to Savannah, in the steamer, St. John, I noticed in the saloon, a fine looking colored girl, who had all the care, or "minded" a very troublesome child, of about a year old, that belonged to her mistress. All day long, with the most untiring patience, without hardly a moment's respite, did she, a child—for she was not more than twelve or fourteen—care for her infant charge. By 11 o'clock P. M., the parents and child, were all nicely fixed for a good sleep, in a magnificent state room. But no thought or care was given, to provide a place of rest for that weary child, who had been so faithful to her task all day, and relieved the mother of so much labor.

She walked wearily up and down the saloon, for a few moments, rolling her big, expressive eyes from side to side, as if in doubt what to do. She was among strangers, and evidently, in new circumstanccs. She finally returned to the state room door of her mistress, and in a most graceful attitude, which would have been a study for an artist, curled or crouched down, leaned her head against the door, and was soon, we hope, in the land of dreams, of sunshine, and song.

CHAPTER XVI.

A STRANGE THING.

Is it not strange, that a system that allows the most unheard of cruelties to be practised, upon four millions of native born Americans, barbarities that the tongue would fain refuse to speak, and the pen to utter, is not at once condemned, by every follower of the meek and lowly Saviour? That there are persons and presses, to apologise for, and defend Slavery, most strikingly illustrates how familiarity with wrong, can paralyse the conscience to all sense of guilt—so that, having eyes, we see not, and ears, we hear not, the groans and cries for help, that fill the air around us.

A heathen writer truthfully remarks, "That the gods gave us a fearful power, when they gave us the faculty of becoming *accustomed* to things."

It is past all question, that in the Free States, the great source and fountain of our crime, poverty, tears, and wretchedness—results from the retailing of ardent apirits. And yet, we have become so accustomed to the traffic, that most communities allow it, either more or less openly.

I shall, perhaps, never forget the impression made on my mind, in the city of M., of the first sale of human beings, that I ever witnessed. I had read of such things for yəars, but now, the reality was before me. A noble looking man, nearly white, was first ordered to mount the auction block, that all might estimate the amount of labor, those bones and muscles might perform. And then his place was occupied with a mother, whose countenance betokened the deepest sorrow, holding a beautiful child of three years old, by the hand. It was with difficulty, that I could restrain myself from mounting the auction block by her side, and in such burning words, as I might have been able to use, denounced a scene, that the sun might blush to look upon. I looked around, to see if others shared my feelings; but it was an everyday sight with them. They evinced no more feeling, than if it had been a sale of cattle or mules.

As I walked away, I hardly dared to look anybody in the face; for it seemed as if I had been guilty of some great crime, in even witnessing such a sight. I seemed less of a man than before. Perhaps, one caught stealing sheep, would not have felt much worse, or more disgraced. But after witnessing such scenes for months, I could realize something why it was, that there was so little feeling among the bystanders, in the case referred to.

Is it not owing, in part, to this hardening influence of familiarity, which leads so many, from the North, to become slaveholders, after a short residence at the South?

The evil has so long existed among us, that the conscience of the Nation, respecting the humanity, and the rights of the colored man, has been well nigh destroyed. We should as soon think of cutting off our right hand, as of depriving the English, the Irish, German, or Frenchman, of those privileges and rights, which, without any scruples or qualms of conscience, we coolly take from the Negro.

Truly has one eloquently said, "We have got used to things that might stir the dead in their graves."

When but a tithe of the wrongs, the slave daily endures, has been made known in England, France, Germany, down-trodden Italy, there has been a perfect shriek and outcry of horror. America alone remains cool, and piously lifting up her blood-red hands, asks, "What is the matter?" Europe answers back, "Why, we have heard that men, women and children are sold in your country like cattle."

"Of course they are," says America; "but what then?"

"We have heard," says Europe, "that in your professedly Christian nation, you have millions, that you keep, by fines and imprisonment, from reading the Bible."

"We know that," says America; "but what *is* this outcry about?"

"We have heard," says Europe, "that Christian girls are sold for purposes of shame, under the very shadow of your tallest steeples, with not a word of rebuke from those who minister in the pulpit!"

"'Tis even so," says America; "but still, what is this *excitement* about?"

"We hear that four millions of your people can have no legal, or scriptural marriage tie," says Europe.

"Certainly, we admit all that," returns America; "but you made such an outcry, we thought you saw some *great cruelty*, or *moral wrong* going on."

"And you profess to be a free and Christian country!" says indignant Europe.

"Of course *we are*, the *freest* and most *enlightened* country in the world; what are you talking about?" says America.

"You send your missionaries to christianize us," says Turkey, "and our religion has abolished this horrible system."

"You! you are all heathen over there—what right haye you to talk, or ask questions?" answers America, evidently becoming too much excited to allow of any further conversation.

CHAPTER XVII.

SOMETHING MORE STRANGE.

PERHAPS nothing in my Southern tour, astonished me more, than to find, universally, that the poor class of whites, upon whom the curse of Slavery seems to rest with greater weight, than even on the slaves themselves; bearing its burthens, but enjoying none of its advantages, should be the most ferocious, and vehement advocates of Slavery to be found. The situation of tens of thousands of slaves, so far as physical comforts are concerned, is altogether preferable. The poor whites are ground to powder, between the upper and nether millstones of its power. And yet, of all persons, they are the least disposed to listen to any argument for the abolishing of Slavery. And if a mob is wanted, to drive from the community, any one suspected of abolition sentiments, it can be raised at a moment's notice, by appealing to this class.

Mrs. Stowe gives this as a reason:

> "They feel the scorn of the upper classes, and their only means of consolation is, in having a class below them, whom they may scorn in turn. To set the negro at liberty, would deprive them of this last comfort; and, accordingly, no class of men advocate Slavery with such frantic and unreasoning violence, or hate abolitionists with such demoniac hatred."

But I am not willing to take this unfavorable view of human nature.

A gentleman, in South Carolina, who has produced the strongest argument for Slavery, of any that we have seen, gives this explanation of the fact under consideration.

Speaking of the evils, which the poor whites must endure, if the slaves are emancipated, he says:

> "The poor white man will be placed in a condition, incomparably worse, than Slavery itself. His labor would come in competition with negro labor. They would be placed on terms of perfect equality with the negro race: except that the negroes would impose on them, and assert their own superiority. For the work to be done, they would be rivals and competitors of each other, and become natural enemies. The negroes being more numerous and powerful than the poor white man, they would oppress and impose on him, and he would become, practically, the slave of the negro race, and could only free himself from this condition, by leaving the home of his childhood, the land that gave him birth, or, by a slaughter of the negro race, or being slaughtered himself."

If the owners of slaves, have taken pains to make the poor whites believe in such sophistries, and they have been deceived by such reasoning, it is not so much a cause of wonder, that the four millions of non slave holders, should take sides with the three hundred and fifty thousand, who live upon the toil and sweat of unrequited labor.

But it is a sad sight, to see these poor whites, in utter ignorance of the blessings of Free Soil, and Free Labor, toiling, to make stronger, their own fetters, and to increase the weight of those burthens, which are crushing them to the earth. Their condition is now, the worst possible, for they are, in a certain sense, the slaves of slaves.

With these two explanations, of this very strange fact, by two intelligent persons, one from the North, the other from the South, I leave my readers to adopt either opinion, or propose a theory, which may account more truthfully, for the cause of that love, which the poor whites bear to the system of Slavery.

I will, however, give the opinion of a poor white, a cracker, of North Carolina, that never had owned any negroes, and never intended to. When asked what he thought about emancipating negroes—

"Well, I'll tell you what I think on it; I'd like it, if we could get rid on 'em to yonst; I wouldn't like to have 'em freed, if they was going to hang around. They ought to get some country, and put 'em war they would be by themselves. It wouldn't do any good to free 'em, and let 'em hang round, because they is so monstrous lazy; if they hadn't got no body to take keer of 'em, you see they wouldn't do nothin' but juss nat'rally laze round, and steal, and pilfer, and no man couldn't live. That's one objection, and this ere's the other. Now suppose they was free, you see, they'd all think themselves just as good as we; of course they would, if they was free. Now, just suppose you had a family of children, how would you like to have a nigger feelin' just as good as a white man? How'd you like to have a nigger stepping up to your darter? Of course you wouldn't; and that's the reason I wouldn't like to hev 'em free; but I tell you, I don't think its right to hev 'em slaves so, that's the fac, taint right to keep 'em as they is."

CHAPTER XVIII.

A WAYSIDE FLOWER.

At the close of a weary day's tramp, through the woods of western Georgia, I turned aside to seek shelter in a rude log cabin, standing at a short distance from the road.

A little girl, of some twelve years, answered my call at the door, and invited me in. Her dress was of the plainest kind: but she was blessed with one of those expressive, speaking, winning countenances that at once, take the beholder captive.

She courteously offered me a rude seat, before a blazing light wood fire, in the genial warmth of which, three or four white children, and one very black, were basking, under her care. On my inquiry, she said her mother would be in soon, and at once engaged in conversation, with all the ease and propriety, of any Northern girl of her years, who might have enjoyed the best of advantages.

I was only the more astonished, as I learned the privilege of schools had not been hers, except to a very limited degree. Her father, like thousands of other, "Sand Hillers," and Piney Woods men, could not read. His grandfather had sent him two quarters to learn to dance; but not one day to learn the useless art of reading.

After supper, it was some how made known, that she possessed some knowledge of music. And, at my request, without any of the affectation of our fashionable singers, "that she had a bad cold—or was out of voice," she produced her note book, and sang away, most sweetly, for an hour or more, like one of the mocking birds, that fill her own native woods with melody. Weary with travel, a thousand miles from loved friends, I listened to that wild warbler, with feelings I never knew before.

In the morning, I observed the cabin was hung round with flowers, which she had painted on all sorts of paper, with such paints as she had been able to manufacture from berries, and other things, which the woods produced.

It was then, that I wished for wealth, to take her from her obscure situation, and put her in a position, to improve, to their fullest extent, those powers of mind, which had been given to her, above many.

CHAPTER XIX.

MISSISSIPPI BOTTOMS IN ARKANSAS.

In regard to these Bottoms, we have to say, they are composed of the richest land in the world, more or less overflowed at high water; covered with a most majestic growth of timber, vines, impenetrable cane-brakes, and whatever of vegetation, a rich, moist soil, and warm sun can produce. Persons too poor to buy land east of the Mississippi, come and squat on government land, and live at their ease, suiting themselves as to the time of payment.

It is the resort also of Freebooters, who have been driven out of good society, on the other side of the river; for here every man is a law to himself, doing what is right in his own eyes, redressing his own wrongs, having no fear of courts or sheriffs. Homicides and murders are no uncommon occurrences. It may truly be called the "dark and bloody ground."

Here is the paradise of hunters, and the place to live at ease. The woods are overstocked with the finest game, and the water courses literally covered, during the winter, with every kind of water fowl, who spend their summers far away in the northern zone.

A few days' labor with the axe, rears a comfortable habitation, for that warm climate. Not a pane of glass is needed, and a few nails, for the doors, is all that is necessary, besides his own labor.

The fire-place is built of earth, taken from the side of his cabin, moulded into the desired shape, very much after the manner of building concrete houses, which soon dries to a brick like hardness.

No labor is needed to provide forage for stock.

They range at will, in summer, and in winter, grow fat in the cane brakes. Their pork is fattened upon the mast in the woods, finished off, if they choose, with a little corn. In regard to fuel, the only difficulty is, there is *too much* of it.

An acre or two girdled, and planted with corn, provides them with bread; for the word, wheat, is not in their vocabulary. The finest of sweet potatoes are raised in the greatest abundance. And if they choose to put in an acre or two of cotton, to have something to buy coffee, powder, whiskey, and some other things considered necessary; they are in first rate, independent circumstances.

The most common pet of the ladies, in that vicinity, is a tame deer, and nothing can be more gentle or graceful, while the gentlemen, but too often, prefer a tame bear, upon whose friendship, or good behavior, it will not do to trust too confidently, as by one ugly grip of my hand, I found out to my sorrow.

Cotton, instead of being a stinted shrub, of a foot and a half high, as on the worn out plantations of the Carolinas and Georgia, grows to a tree like size, causing no bending of the negroe's back, in the picking.

And now, lest some learning these facts, and having grown nearly desperate, with oft-returning rent days, and quarterly presentation of butcher's and grocer's bills, with a purse, constantly in a state of collapse, should sigh for a free home, in the wild woods of Arkansas, I ought to state, that the inhabitants, though so highly favored in some respects, yet have a terrible battle to fight, during three or four months of the year, with chills and fever, and kindred diseases. Before going, it might be well to count the cost, whether a more healthy climate, and much hard work, had better be exchanged for a life of freedom from severe labor, but a greater liability to sickness and consequent suffering.

CHAPTER XX.

THE AUTHOR PREACHES THE GOSPEL IN THAT REGION; RIDES, OR RATHER, WALKS HIS CIRCUIT.

Hearing much of the great need of ministerial labor, among the Squatters on those Bottoms, I resolved to volunteer my services, and labor for a while among them; thinking it would be the more acceptable, as the preachers were absent at Conference, and would not return for a month or more.

I was ferried from the east to the west side of the Mississippi, landed in the woods, put upon a trail, which I was to boldly follow, ten miles due west, when I should come to a, "one horse county town," where I could obtain some definite directions of the circuit I was to travel.

It was past meridian, and my hope was, to arrive there in season to pass the night.

The day was one of the most beautiful that autumn can furnish; and with a light heart, I pressed vigorously forward. It was a feast to the eyes—to gaze upon those gigantic trees, gum, sycamore, cotton wood, cypress, that had never lacked for sun, or moisture, or depth of earth, and could count their years by centuries. None of your stinted, New England shrubbery, that we call, "woods," of twenty or fifty years' growth, of the five months, in each year, on a soil that contains no nutriment. No! no! no! —far from it. One acre of such timber, if located in the old Bay State, would be a fortune. Vines were trailing from tree to tree, loaded with delicious grapes, while the woods were vocal with the song of birds, who, on their way from their northern home, to a more sunny clime, were tarrying for a while, in this El Dorado, feasting, at will, upon the good things, that a kind Providence, had so liberally provided for them.

Now and then, often enough to change the scene, we came upon the log cabin of a Squatter, who had opened up a space to the sunlight, and planted it with corn, which grew so luxuriantly, that we could by no means reach the ears.

A little before sunset, we arrived at the "Town," consisting of a grocery, where rum, whiskey, and tobacco were the main articles for sale ; a blacksmith's shop, post office, court house, on a very small scale, and a jail to correspond. These, with a few log cabins, made up the embryo city.

Upon inquiry, we found that the keeper of the rum doggery, was the official representative of the religion of the place, and in whose house the ambassadors of the Cross were expected to be entertained.

We turned aside, and knocked boldly at the door of his cabin, which, like all others in that region, was raised about three feet from the ground, on posts, furnishing a fine shelter, and common play ground for young negroes, dogs, pigs, and lame ducks,

No sooner had we rapped, than our right leg was seized, a little below the knee, and held, as in a vice, by a blood hound, that sprang from his lair, under the house. What the result might have been, we know not, if the lady, at that moment. had not appeared at the door, and rescued us, with only the suffering of severe flesh wounds, and a sad rending of our unmentionables.

Without expressing any sympathy at my condition, or suggesting any way in which my clothing could be repaired, so that we might appear decently among strangers, she strongly intimated, that I ought to apologise to the dog, for having intruded on his premises; "that I should have stood in the road, and hallooed to the house, signifying that I wished to come in; that the dog had been learned to give a *death grip* to every thing that passed the gate."

I, of course, begged hers, and the dog's pardon, and hoped that the fact, that I was a stranger in Arkansas—having been less than twelve hours in the State—and unacquainted with their method of receiving outsiders, would be considered by both, a sufficient apology.

But I inwardly resolved, that if such were the customs and manners of Arkansas, I would, with as little delay as possible, provide myself with some lead pills, and an instrument for administering them, which I did not fail to do, a short time after.

Not being very well pleased with my reception, and the language of the lady bearing too close a relation to that used in a certain, "fish market," I did not ask to share her hospitality; but only if she could direct me to some family, who could take me in for the night.

She referred me to the wife of the jailor, to whose house, I repaired at once, and received a Christian welcome.

About eight o'clock, a low whistle was heard on the outside of the cabin, when the jailor at once arose, and took his hat, telling his wife, to put the stranger to bed at the proper time.

After he left, she remarked, with a sigh, that "he had gone to the court house, (the key to which he kept) to spend most of the night with a company of gamblers, who used the county property for that purpose."

Her dwelling was, perhaps, sixteen feet square. Three beds occnpied three corners of the room. Near the fourth corner, was the fire place, on one side, and a table and window on the other.

The evening was passed pleasantly in conversation, the room being lighted as brilliantly as Aladdin's Palace, from a, "light wood" fire, (pitch pine knots). When near the time of retiring, God's word was read, and prayer offered. She then pointed to the bed I was to occupy, but gave no indications of leaving the room.

I soon concluded, that I was in a place, where necessity and custom, did not consider the presence of a lady, any objection to a gentleman's disrobing, and safely esconcing himself between the sheets; which we did, in about as short a space of time, as we were ever known to perform a similar feat.

Soon she took one of the other beds, and we talked till, perhaps, near twelve o'clock. In short, I only dared to go to sleep with one eye, fearing, lest the husband might return, the worse for liquor, and his bowie knife be placed in unpleasant proximity to my ribs.

And not till he had returned, and was safely in the right bed,.did I dare to close both eyes, and sink into the embrace of sleep,—

"Sleep, balmy sleep, nature's sweet restorer."

Early the next morning, having obtained all needed directions for my course, and leaving an appointment for a future Sabbath, I was on my way, and before night, came into the neighborhood, where one of the sermons, on the following Sabbath, was to be delivered. Word was sent out in different directions, to the neighbors, dwelling within eight or twelve miles; for in that country, that distance is no obstacle to attendance upon church.

The building would seat comfortably, perhaps, fifty or seventy-five persons, and was as rudely constructed as their own dwellings. Not a pane of glass in it.

Holes were cut through at intervals, for light and ventilation.

On those slab seats, untouched with a smoothing plane, and rejoicing in no backs, the rich and the poor were alike welcome.

We had great liberty in speaking; the most undivided attention was given to the word; and we were led to ask, whether a sacrifice more acceptable to God, was not offered, on that occasion, than by many a fashionable congregation, sitting on cushioned seats, worshipping in a temple, which, in some respects, might vie with that built by Solomon.

Their readiness to overcome obstacles, that they might attend, was strikingly in contrast, with the dwellers in our cities, From bridle paths, leading into the forest, on different sides, a lady, on horseback, would be seen approaching the church, with a child, a few months old, in her arms. One, a little more than two years of age, would be clinging to the mane in front, while another, of more than four years, was safely enthroned behind. The husband, with true fatherly pride, walks by their side, and was a safe guide for the way.

The service being closed, a horse was provided, and with a hunter for my guide, we struck into the woods, to gain the next appointment, some ten miles distant, which we somewhat shortened, by a route, that my guide knew, marked by, " blazed trees."

That appointment had been shunned for some time, by the circuit preacher, because a widow lady, of somewhat doubtful character, and her little children, having no other shelter, had entered the church, and taken possession of one corner, with her bed, stove, and a few housekeeping utensils of the plainest kind, leaving plenty of room for the congregation that ordinarily assembled. We could not think the preacher was justified in forsaking the, " appointment." because this woman, wtth her innocent children, had taken refuge in the sanctuary of the Lord.

We did not fail to exhort her, that dw· lling thus in His house, she ought to be distinguished for goodness, and purity of character.

After the services were closed, the hunter, who had been my guide during the day, joined by his comrade, invited me to enjoy hunter's fare with them, at their cabin in the dense forest. Having no other invitation, we accepted. The horse was left, and starting into an Indian lope, we held on our course, as rapidly as the obstructions of the way would allow. Just at dusk, the wigwam was gained, a rude structure, nine feet by fifteen, made of cypress, rived with the axe, and so free was the timber, that it bore a close resemblance to boards. The lower ends were driven into the ground, and the upper lashed to a pole, supported by a forked stick, roofed with the same.

Two days' work made for these men, a comfortable and happy home, far away from the strife of tongues. Their rifles procured them an abundance of the finest game. A few days' labor would raise all the corn necessary for their bread. The scalps of wolves, and the skins of beasts, procuring what few necessaries they needed.

Hungry and tired, we threw ourselves upon a bed of bear skins, in the corner, to await supper. A blazing fire being kindled, made the interior light and cheerful.

Before it was soon swinging, a fat raccoon, of enormous size, which they had secured the day before, whose flesh, they assured me, I should find, in the eating, "to equal the finest shoat I ever tasted." Generous slices of vension were taken from over head, and with bear's fat, to supply the place of butter, in the cooking utensil, the exhalations from which, added to that of the roasting coon, and a coffee pot supplied liberally with the best Mocha, steaming on the hot coals, filled the cabin; giving unmistakable evidence, to a hungry man, of the rich feast that was preparing. That fine loaf pone bread, the invariable attendant of every meal at the South, with none of those condiments, which northern cooks apply, yet surpassing theirs in flavor, made of only two things—meal and water, was placed in the old fashioned bake-kettle, which the modern stove has displaced, ready to be served up warm, with the other, "fixings." Sweet potatoes were stowed away in the embers and hot ashes. Last, but not least, splendid honey, from the hollow trees of the surrounding forest.

A cedar slab served for a table, which fairly groaned with the weight of the good cheer, which the wilderness had provided for us. In due time, we gathered around it, on rude stools, and we doubt whether, from snow white damask, on Sevre's porcelain, with silver service, and costly chandeliers flashing over us, we ever enjoyed a better supper.

The desert consisted of the finest grapes, with which, the trees around, were literally loaded. There being no third service to attend, supper was protracted to a somewhat late hour.

In the meanwhile, the clouds that had been gathering, during the whole afternoon, began to pour out their contents. The wind increased to a fierce tempest, roaring above us like the tread of an earthquake. The monarchs of that ancient forest, threw their mighty arms wildly about, striking against each other, with fearful crash, as though struggling for life, in a deadly and unequal contest with an unseen enemy. Now and then, a crackling, crashing peal, reverberating through the woods, like distant thunder, announced that the work of destruction was going on.

The wolves ran howling from their coverts. But while all was so dark, fearful, and dismal without, we had peace and joy within, as before a blazing fire, we sang the songs of Zion, and in prayer, committed ourselves to the care of Him, who hath promised that his people, "shall dwell safely in the wilderness, and sleep in the woods."

During some of the wakeful hours of that night, amid the howling of the storm, and the serenade of wolves, among other reflections, we were led to consider, how little, in reality, man *really needs* to make him happy.

Here, in the depths of this forest, were two men, whose entire establishment, save their rifles, might be purchased for fifteen dollars, enjoying more, of all that makes life desirable, than the owner of many a splendid establishment, in our great cities, which cost, with its fixings, more than one hundred thousand dollars. Should one answer curtly, "That there was no wife to support in their case," we reply, one of them told me, that as soon as he had a day of more leisure, he intended to add an extra room to his establishment, and invite one of the ladies, of that vicinity, to preside over it. And if I could only tarry a week or two longer, I should have the honor of performing the marriage ceremony. So different were the habits of the ladies in that region, from those of our city belles, that we think he would find his expenses not much increased; while the general order, neatness, and comfort of the establishment, with the magic power of a neat womau, to preside over it, would be increased an hundred fold.

For a few days, we enjoyed greatly, the hospitality of these men; having a quiet time for writing in their cabin, while they were abroad with their rifles, realizing the affirmative of the question, asked by the Psalmist, that "God can furnish a table in the wilderness." After visiting the sick in that region, holding meetings in different settlements, we bid them farewell, and obtaining directions, started for the next Sabbath appointment of the circuit.

But as the manners, customs, and way of living were very much the same, we need not detain the reader any longer. The first week's experience in Arkansas, was often repeated with slight variations. What I have narrated, will give some idea of frontier life in that region.

We learned, that many things, that we had thought necessary to our happiness, were not strictly needed. And that one half of the world, does not know how the other half lives.

Though sleeping often without doors or windows, and always serenaded with wolves, we never enjoyed better rest. Nor did we ever preach the gospel with greater liberty and freedom, or to those, who seemed more anxious to receive it. Hardly a day has passed since, but we have longed for the privilege again, of preaching the gospel, to the dwellers in the grand old woods of Arkansas.

CHAPTER XXI.

HUMAN NATURE THE SAME, WHETHER BLACK OR WHITE.

Many a lady in the Free States, remains unmarried, for a time, at least, because those that offer themselves, do not suit her fancy. It is so among the poor slaves.

A negro in Georgia told me, that, "a good many of the girls, on their plantation, were not married, because they did not consider the boys smart enough for them."

In the cities, there is as much of an aristocracy among the slaves, as among the whites. And one of them would be as much disgraced, to associate, or marry out of that rank, as their masters or mistresses. They have their, "Fifth Avenue" assemblies, or dress balls, got up without any regard to expense.

The cards of invitation, are handsomely engraved, and duly embossed.

There are regular masters of ceremonies, floor committees, &c. Ladies are assured that they can depend on the most perfect order being observed. And all goes, "merry as a marriage bell."

No Broadway exquisite, can do the agreeable to the ladies, in any better style, than is done by these colored gentlemen of the first circle.

A supper, as good as money can furnish, abounding, besides the substantials, with the various wines, ice cream in abundance, with all the rich flavored fruits of the tropical zone, is a part of the evening's entertainment.

For a Northerner, or one unacquainted with such facts of slave life, to look in upon that scene, and witness the display of jewelry, of silks and satins, and Honiton lace, of white kids, and costly fans ; the flirtations with, and coquetish smiles from behind them, countenances of such perfect beauty, that these ornaments seem hardly a fit accompaniment, faultless forms, with a grace and elasticity of motion, never seen, but with perfect health. I say, one out of slave land, could hardly realize, that the fairest, and most Hebe like of those ladies, the one whose beauty was most peerless, might, in conformity with the majesty of the law, be on the auction block, by ten o'clock of the following day, to be sold to the highest bidder. To be added to the Harem of the buyer, or placed in the water, mud, and miasma of the rice field, under a brutal overseer, just as a nod from the owner of God's beautiful workmanship should determine.

Thus, full of striking contrasts, is slave life. It would be hard to believe, that those poor, degraded, care-worn females, with hardly rags enough to cover them, that with hoe or axe in hand, most laboriously toiling, we passed, as we entered the city, are the sisters, belong to the same race, of those in that gay assembly room. That both are alike slaves, and are liable to be sold like a mule in the market.

We were saying, that human nature is the same in the black and white man. We have seen it true in regard to love, and fondness for display in dress, we see it also, in connection with religious duties.

A colored sexton in Memphis, was congratulating, on his recent marriage, one of the former pastors of the church. After a round of well expressed good wishes for his happiness, the minister thanked him, and kindly inquired, how he was prospering in his religious life. Whether he was really in the enjoyment of religion?

Cuffee said, "he had thought much about religion, and had tried to get it; and, in short, believed, he had obtained, all but the *substance*."

Many white persons, we fear, would have to make a similar confession, of lacking the *substance*, if they were equally simple and truthful.

Conversing one day with a slave, who had brought a load of cotton to market, on the subject of religion, he acknowledged its importance, said he meant to get it."

Then why do you not? said I.

"Well, it 'pears like, they keep me driving steers so much, I can't."

How many white persons, are driving so earnestly, business, or pleasure, as to have no time to attend to religion.

CHAPTER XXII.

WHAT HAS THE NORTH TO DO WITH SLAVERY?

MUCH, every way. One need not be in the South more than three months, to see the foolishness of the question, so often asked by Northern dough-faces, "Why do you talk about emancipation in the Free States? Why not go South, where Slavery exists?"

Of nothing am I more strongly convinced, than that Slavery will die, when the North takes right ground on this great question.

Besides its elements of strength, found in man's natural love of power, it has elements of weakness, which would cause its speedy death, were it not for the moral support it receives from the inhabitants of the Free States. In them, where free discussion is allowed, the whole battle can be fought. Millions of Northern capital is, invested in slaves.

Thousands of our young men, yearly go South, to engage in business, teach school, or in some professional employment, and with not so much conscience as those born under the system, they become slaveholders, and not unfrequently, out Herod, Herod himself in brutal treatment.

It was continually thrown in my face, "that the Yankee had no conscience,—that all he cared for, was to make money; and if he could make money by holding slaves, he would do it, "a leetle" quicker, than any body else.

I knew that there was but too much truth in the assertion.

The *spirit* of slaveholding exists, far too strongly, at the North, if the thing itself does not, and cannot be too earnestly rebuked.

One of our leading, religious journals, professing to be truly Anti-Slavery, some time since, in an article on, "the trials of an house-keeper," said, in substance, as follows. The writer, evidently a lady, complained, "that her hired girl, dressed so tidy, as to be not unfrequently mistaken for the lady of the house. That she was so cultivated, as to be able to appreciate Shakespeare, and other old standard English authors, of world wide fame.—Complained that she wrote letters on fine note paper, enclosed in embossed envelopes, and directed with a taste and beauty of penmanship, that her mistress could not hope to equal. And that she should have presumed to ask some of the gentlemen of the house, whose business called them past the post office, to drop them in for her. Or when so tired as to not be able to take another step, she had ventured to pass through the front door, instead of going way back, some round about way, through the kitchen."

That woman, or person, who could write in that style, only needs to have the power, and she would make another, "Mrs. St. Clair," of the worst kind. Such an one, has a heart, to grind down, and oppress the poor, the laboring class, without any regard to color. Why, I always supposed, that pure religion, and our common humanity, bid us rejoice in the cultivation of those below us. That it is a glorious thing, when they are so educated, as to appreciate the English classics, and write a good hand, and not to be condemned, when they have a desire to appear neat and tidy about their work.

Doubtless, she would rejoice, if each of her servants, were obliged to wear some badge, by which it might be known everywhere, that they belonged to the working, or serving class.

And we are not able to see, wherein it was so great a wrong, as to be worthy of a newspaper philippic; that a domestic, taking some of her hard earned money, enclosing it to her widowed mother, to supply her necessities, and not being allowed time to go to the office herself, should respectfully ask a gentleman of the house, to do it for her.

We have but too many unreasonable, Marie St. Clair's, all over the Free States. Human nature is no worse at the South, than at the North. We only have this advantage, that the laws restrain us, to a certain extent, and keep us back from that physical violence, which, I fear, many, in moments of passion, would be ready to inflict, or have done to order.

How many have we, that prefer Irish, or German servants, or foreign born, because, from their ignorant, or dependent condition, they will bear a treatment, that no intelligent, native born American, would, for a moment submit too?

A writer, from the Southern stand point of observation, might collect facts of the treatment of domestics, in even the christian families of the North, which would be most startling.

Words may be so applied, to the sensitive nature of our domestics, as to cause more of real pain, and lasting anguish, than the lash upon the bleeding back.

Let us take the beam from our own eye, before we say too much about the mote in anothers. And let us never forget, that it is a part of true religion, as well as of republicanism, to do all that we can, to raise those below us, to our own standard of intelligence.

We never need to fear, the expending too much labor on this object.

The South is extremely sensitive to the public opinion of the North ; and when that is right, Slavery will melt away before it, like snow, before an April sun. The more intelligent of the Southern people, read Northern books and papers ; they keep tolerably well posted up, in regard to that great change, which is moving on so rapidly in the Free States.

They tremble in view of the hour, evidently so near, when all outside of Slavery, shall be united against it. It is an old proverb, "that a guilty conscience finds accusers in stones." This was verified in the fact, that a slave holder, who had visited Mount Auburn, complained to me, most bitterly, that the fanaticism of the North, should have erected a marble monument, to the martyr Torrey, who so sadly perished in a Southern prison, for having shown practical sympathy for the poor slave. But we say, let our hills, and vallies, heaven and earth, testify against this relic of barbarism, till it retreats from the face of the earth.

They appear like persons ill at ease, over sensitive, that strangers should have a favorable opinion, of the, "peculiar institution."

Almost, or quite the first question, after an introduction, is something like this : "Well, you have seen something of Slavery, I 'spose, since you have been in the South, and changed your opinion, have you not? You find it not near as bad as you thought it was, before you left the North, do you not?"

In scores of instances, within five minutes after forming an acquaintance, would we be engaged in an intense discussion on some aspect of the Slavery question. It always being introduced by them, and not by myself.

Every year, they feel the pressure, more and more of a right state of public opinion in the non-slaveholding States.

Of course it could not be otherwise, but in this day of the rapid transmission of news by mail, and of going to and fro of persons for business or pleasure, but that contiguous States, would act, and react on each other. The beneficent influence of free institutions, passes over into slave territory, and like leaven, is silently at work. While the baneful influence of theirs, passes over the line to us. Let one travel in that part of Iowa, bordering on Missouri, the South part of Illinois, Indiana, Pennsylvania, and, unless prepared by a previous knowledge of the facts, he would be completely astounded at the Pro-Slavery spirit, which there prevails.

There is not near that prejudice against color, at the South, as at the North. We venture to affirm, that in no slave holding city, would such an incident have occurred, as took place in Boston, April, 1856, viz: Two young, colored, christian girls, nearly white, were turned out of an ice cream and confectionery saloon, whither they had gone to spend their money for nice things, as any body else would. O! shame, where is thy blush!

CHAPTER XXIII.

PIETY OF THE SLAVES.

We were at no little pains, to make inquiries on this point. Attending their meetings constantly on the Sabbath, and during the week. Conversing with them personally, in regard to their religious experience, as opportunity offered. We wished to ascertain, whether, "Uncle Tom," of world wide fame, was a myth, a mere creation of the imagination, or whether such persons were scattered through the South. We desired to know, whether, as a class, the slaves gave as genuine evidence of piety, of having met with a change of heart, as those of the white race.

I questioned the owners of slaves, their pastors, those having every opportunity to become acquainted with the subject, and invariably received but one answer, viz: to endorse them most fully. Of course, many among them, that make a profession, will only run well for a season. But this is so among the whites. Let equal numbers of white and black be taken, and I was assured, the latter would not suffer by the comparison. As a race, I believe they are more likely to be influenced by religious truth, when brought in contact with it, than the whites.

There is not, with them, so much pride of opinion, they are more docile, teachable, affectionate, than the Anglo Saxon. "And hence, the divine graces of love and faith, when inbreathed by the Holy Spirit, find, in their natural temperament, a more congenial atmosphere."

There is, no doubt, this good result from the strong government of Slavery, that their wills having been broken, subdued, yielded to the masters authority, when they come to learn the higher claims, that their Master in heaven has for their love, their obedience, it is yielded at once, with less of rebellion and opposition.

We see the same principle illustrated every day among the whites. Where strict, family government is maintained, and the children taught to obey promptly, they will be far more likely to yield to the claims of Jesus Christ.

We think the negro has been wronged, by applying the same mathematical rules to his religious experience, that we do to the cool, phlegmatic white race. We lose sight of their tropical origin. Of their oriental character. They have most susceptible temperaments, a vivid fancy and imagination, and are easily moved to tears, or smiles; and when excited, body and soul sympathize together, and there will be, what seem to us, most violent, and uncalled for, physical manifestations. To see in a crowded chapel, towards the close of an animated sermon, from ten to twenty, jumping enormously high, throwing their arms wildly about, with eyes glaring, as if entranced, shouting at the top of their voices, like so many Eastern Dervishes, and then falling almost senseless from exhaustion, would frighten most that might be looking on for the first time.

Some would doubtless say, that this bodily exercise, profiteth little. But let us not forget the words of the Apostle:—"There are diversities of gifts, but the same spirit. There are differences of administrations, but the same Lord. There are diversities of operations, but it is the same God which worketh all in all."

Many from the North, think these manifestations

of religious feeling, entirely uncalled for, and out of place, and wonder how their pastors can allow it.

Many have attempted to repress these exhibitions, to steady the ark, among the blacks. But it has seemed to result in a loss of spiritual power.

A Southern minister, doubtless, took the right view of it, when answering an objector, he said:

"Sir, I am satisfied the races are so essentially different, that they can not be regulated by the same rules. I, at first, felt as you do; and, though I saw that genuine conversions did take place, with all this outward manifestation, I was still so much annoyed by it, as to forbid it among my negroes, till I was satisfied that the repression of it, was a serious hindrance to religious feeling, and then I became certain that all men cannot be regulated in their religious exercises, by one model. I am assured that conversions, produced with these accessories, are quite as apt to be genuine, and to be as influential over the heart and life, as those produced in any other way."

The result, the effect must be the true test by which this question is to be decided, whether among black or white.

A rich planter erected a very neat chapel for his slaves, with a comfortable back rail, to rest the body against, during divine service. But, by and by, his negroes petitioned him to remove it, assigning, as a reason, "that it did not leave them *room enough to pray.*" I have seen them, when it seemed as if limb and life was endangered, by a violent contact with this back rail.

Like all who profess religion, they must be judged by their fruits, their daily walk and conversation. And when we turn to their christian life, their forgivness of injuries; their sterling honesty and devotion to the interests of their masters, without recompense or reward; their attendance upon the means of grace, after hours of weary labor; their cheerful contributions to the cause of Christ, from their hard earnings; their devotion to the sick and suffering, when the Yellow Fever, or the Cholera is around them; their happy, and triumphant deaths, I think we must conclude, that if Christ has any true followers in the world, many of them are to be found among the poor slaves of the South.

The tallest, the blackest, the most gigantic proportioned, and best specimen of the African race, that I met with in all the South, belonged to Mr. ———, of Vicksburg. Mrs. H. B. Stowe's magnificent description of, "Dred," might be applied to him, in every particular, even as if he had sat for the portrait. He must have been Dred's brother.

At church, as they rose to sing, he at once attracted my attention, standing head and shoulders above his fellows, holding his hymn book firmly before him, he sung with that emphasis and power, which demonstrated what delight he took in that part of divine service.

To hear his voice, so strong and clear, pouring out his full soul in strains of richest melody, brought fresh to my mind, these beautiful words of Longfellow:

"Loud he sang the psalm of David!
He, a negro and enslaved,
Sang of Israel's victory,
Sang of Zion, bright and free.

In the hour, when night is calmest,
Sang he from the Hebrew Psalmist,
In a voice so sweet and clear,
That I could not choose but hear,

Songs of triumph, and ascriptions,
Such as reached the swart Egyptians,
When upon the Red Sea coast,
Perished Pharaoh and his host.

And the voice of his devotion,
Filled my soul with strong emotion :
For its tones by turns were glad,
Sweetly solemn, wildly sad.

Paul and Silas, in their prison,
Sang of Christ, the Lord arisen,
And an earthquake's arm of might,
Broke their dungeon gates at night.

But alas ! what holy angel
Brings the Slave this glad evangel?
And what earthquake's arm of might,
Breaks his dungeon gates at night ?"

Towards the close of the service, when the excitement began to be somewhat wild and stormy around him, the influence came upon him. He began to shout, and to jump, in a most rapid, violent, and astonishing manner. It appeared as if he was about to go up, bodily, towards heaven. And it seemed as if his companions feared it, for they clasped him on every side ; either to detain him, or, if he must go, to take them with him. And such was the power resting upon him, that the latter looked likely to be the result.

All that knew him, had the highest confidence in his piety. And when the Yellow Fever visited that city, and several of the clergymen had died at their post, the whites, as well as colored, welcomed to their bedsides, to engage in acts of devotion, this brother beloved, this prince, and mighty wrestler in prayer.

By and by, he was taken sick, and death seemed near. His pastor visited him, and asked, in regard to the state of his mind, "how he felt then, apparently on the borders of the spirit world ?"

"Well, massa, thank God! when I am sick, *I have nothing else to do but to be sick.* I have made all my preparations before; and when the charriot comes, I shall have nothing to do but to step on board."

It would be well, if others, in the time of health, would make the same preparation. But he lived; God had more work for him to perform.

There was one Amelia Hern, in ———, Florida, in whose humble cabin it was often my privilege to enter, and engage in acts of devotion. She remarked, "though nothing but a poor slave, yet, through crosses and losses, disappointments and trials, I mean to gain a place in bright glory. No matter how hard our task is, it may be twelve, before we are able to retire; yet, we always read and pray, ask God to forgive, protect, and bless. So, also, in the morning, the same."

At another time, she remarked, "the devils, the bad spirits, get in the cabin, and we have to pray hard and long, to get them out, and obtain the visits of the good angels."

Can we doubt, but that if others would use the same means, to drive away and dispel wrong spirits. and tempters from their dwellings, there would be the same glorious results?

This Amelia, was a widow, had an idiotic boy of eighteen years to support, and then must, in some way, earn a certain sum each week, to sustain her young master, in vice and idleness. She was one of the four female slaves he inherited. And, on their hard, unrequited service, he played the gentleman, on a small scale. Was able to be quite an aristocratic loafer, for a, "one horse town."

I shall not soon forget a class meeting I attended, with the slaves in Mobile. Or the testimony that an aged, care-worn sister gave in. As, with her great eyes rolling, throwing her body into all sorts of contortions, sawing the air with arms that were but skin and bone, she poured forth a torrent of wordy eloquence, such as I have seldom heard.

Such was the wild excitement of the moment, and the shouting on every side, that I only retained clearly in my memory, these expressions: "Through kicks, curses, and bruises, through cuts, whips and slashes, starvation, nakedness, imprisonment and fire, partings from husband and children, I am bound for the Kingdom, and expect to see the King in his beauty; and that these feet, weary and blistered with life's travel, shall yet stand on that, 'sea of glass,' and walk the golden streets of the New Jerusalem. And these withered hands, shall pluck the twelve manner of fruits, from those trees, that line the banks of the river of life. O! my dear brethren and sisters, I expect, soon to be in that land, where the last tear shall be wiped away from these eyes, so used to weeping. Where there shall be no more sorrow; nor crying, nor any pain, for former things will all have passed away."

And without any fear of, "lower law men," before my eyes, I uttered a hearty amen! that all this might prove true. And I believe the gates of pearl, will fly open wide, when that heir of glory comes to enter in. And that her name will be enrolled among those, who shall have come, "out of great tribulation, and have washed their robes, and made them white in the blood of the Lamb."

One afternoon, in Natches, in a large church, crowded with negro worshippers, the pastor, instead of preaching, spent the time, in a kind of 'experience meeting." Calling upon different ones, to give in their testimony on the subject of religion.

One aged mother, spoke in substance, as follows:

"I have no desire for concerts, theatres, circuses, &c. No! no! no! Not even to open the door and peak at them, as they go through the streets. Jesus makes music in my soul. I never wakes in the night, but I offers my petitions, that God would convert my wicked children, and revive his work. O, what a blessed contracted meeting we had. (Alluding to a profitable, protracted meeting, held some months before.) "O, what a good contracted meeting that was." Referring to it in this way many times.

An old, grey headed class leader remarked, "Secret prayer is my food. In de closet, is de place, where I gets strengthened for life's journey, its duties, and trials."

I had a most interesting conversation, in South Carolina, with an old, blind, worn out slave, that had been led out into the pines, by a little child, to gather an arm full of wood for his cabin. Among other questions, I asked, why do you love God ?

"'Case he first loved me, and gib his Son to die for me."

How much do you pray ?

"Night and day, ebry hour. I constantly thinks how good God is."

In the testimonies quoted above, we have, certainly, the language of Canaan, of the true, experimental christian. And may we not charitably believe, that having so little to hope for from earth, that many have become truly wise, and have laid up treasure in heaven ? If giving freely is any sign that the heart has been enlarged by the love of God, we have that evidence also. A poor slave, a Baptist, in one of the rice swamps of Carolina, said he would not be afraid to give his last cent to the cause of Christ, for benevolent purposes. He had faith to believe, that God would make it up to him in some manner.

Their contributions are not injured, that way, by being dabbled with by, "Alexander the copper smith," as in Yankee land. One, three, and five cent coin are not so often found in the box. But tens and quarters abound. We saw them so ready to contribute, that if obliged to leave before the service closed, they would step forward, and leave their offering on the communion table. We can, " guess," of some parts of the country, where this would not be done.

In many cities of the South, there are large, colored churches, who support either a white or colored pastor, in a very comfortable, and creditable manner. From their hard earnings, giving a salary, that ought to make many a Free State congregation blush.

In 1853, five thousand slaves, in Charleston, contributed fifteen thousand dollars for benevolent purposes. Where could the same number of white professors of religion be found, whose contributions would average three dollars apiece?

There are some masters and mistresses, at the South, that take commendable pains to furnish religious instruction to their, " people." While the great majority, we are fully convinced, are very criminal in neglecting the religious instruction of souls committed so completely to their charge.

But there is no concealing the fact, that there is untold guilt, out of the slave States, in regard to neglecting the spiritual interests of our domestics. In the cities of the South, thousands are detained at home, most, or all of the Sabbath, to attend to the domestic duties of the family. One service, many of them can attend. The males are more at leisure, and some of them may hear three good sermons.

Viewing the privileges that many enjoy in the city, the author of, " South Side View," as well as others, have given to the inhabitants of the Free States, the most erroneous and untruthful impressions, in regard to the religious privileges, with which the *slaves generally*, are favored. The millions of this servile class, are not in the city, but on plantations. The hearing of a sermon, from an intelligent minister of Jesus Christ, is one of the rare events of the year.

The people are so isolated at the South, that from this cause, if there were no other reason, churches and schools are of very rare occurrence. You travel there scores of miles, without meeting with either. In the Free States, you can hardly be out of sight of one, or the other. They stand like light houses on our hill tops, with their silent fingers pointing to the skies. And they gleam along our vallies, as their most precious adorning. Slavery, a barbarous institution, has made the South, at this day, one vast missionary field. It is ripe for the reaper's hand, but, alas! where are the laborers? Each denomination is asking, imploringly, for help. A few noble hearted men, riding long circuits, absent for weeks from home, are doing what they can to supply this lack of service. Once or twice a month, different parts of the country, have the gospel preached. And if the white, the more favored part of the population, are so poorly supplied with the living ministry, it is easy to infer what must be the condition, of the plantation slaves.

It is not to be expected, that planters, who make no profession of religion, (and they are, by far, in the majority,) are entirely regardless of the interests of their own souls, would be at any very great expense, to provide for the spiritual wants of their negroes.

Meeting a slave boy in the city of ———, whose master I knew, stood high as a christian, in that community, I was curious to know, what privileges he had enjoyed, and what attainments he had made in the knowledge of Bible truth.

He said, in answer to one question, that he was, "thirteen years old." And in respect to another, "that he did not know who came into the world, and died on the cross to save sinners."

Where will you go, when you die?

"Straight to torment."

Why so?

"Dun know to go any where else."

And if knowledge is necessary to salvation, we fear the same sad fate awaits many others.

I have so expressly denied, what Doctor N. Adams, and others, would have the North consider as a fact, viz: that the religious privileges of the slaves, are of a very high order, ("South Side View," p. 53,) that, perhaps, it ought to be sustained by stronger evidence, than my own observation. No one will deny that Slavery in Kentucky, assumes as mild a form as in any of the States. A committee of the Synod of Kentucky, make the following report:

"After making all reasonable allowances, our colored population can be considered, semi-heathen. The law does not recognize the family relations of the Slave, and extends to him no protection in the enjoyments of its endearments. The members of a slave family, may be forcibly separated, so that they shall never more meet till the final judgment. Brothers and sisters, parents and children, husbands and wives, are torn assunder, and permitted to see each other no more. *These acts are constantly occurring in the midst of us.* The shrieks, and the agony often witnessed on such occasions, proclaim, with a trumpet tongue, the iniquity, and the cruelty of our system. *There is not a neighborhood where these heart-rending scenes are not displayed.* There is not a village, or road, that does not behold the sad procession of manacled outcasts, whose chains, and mournful countenances, tell that they are exiled by force from all that the heart holds dear. Our churches, years ago, raised its voice of solemn warning against this flagrant violation of every principle of mercy, justice, and humanity. Yet we blush to announce to you, and to the world, that this warning has been often disregarded, even by those that hold to our communion. *Cases have occurred in our own denomination, where professors of the religion of mercy, have torn the mother from her children, and sent her into a merciless and returnless exile.* Yet, acts of discipline have rarely followed such conduct."

This evidence, from those who reside on the ground, and were personally acquainted with the facts, with no motive to paint, in darker colors, than the truth will bear, must be conclusive.

CHAPTER XXIV.

GOOD WHERE WE SHOULD NOT EXPECT IT.

I SPENT some time in Memphis, a beautiful and enterprising city, in the southwest corner of the State of Tennessee, on the banks of the Mississippi.

The most wicked man in the place, according to human judgment, was one J— A—. He had killed a great many persons, in duels, and personal encounters, in various ways; had been tried many times, for different State prison offences; but he always got clear somehow. He was a professed gambler. I used to meet him often, with his gold headed cane, dressed and looking as respectable as an Alderman. He had a son—a chip of the old block. He made an excursion to California; and in the gambling saloons of San Francisco, soon made his pile of forty thousand, and wisely retired from the theatre of his operations, before he should "break," came back and built a house for his mother and sisters, so that they might have a home, should the father ever meet with reverses.

When the yellow fever—or Death on his pale Horse—was riding through their streets, the sick and the dying everywhere, consternation and fear on every countenance, then this young man, instead of fleeing to the mountains for health, acted the part of the Good Samaritan, and with his carriage, was visiting all around the city, looking up the poor and the suffering, giving food here, and money there, and calling medical help, as it was needed.

Nor can any one, who has never been among those scenes of suffering, caused by the fever, appreciate, fully, such deeds of charity.

In the same city, at the same time, the Memphis Conference, of the M. E. Church, was in session. As they were about to close, they resolved themselves into a Preachers Aid Society, to raise money, for the widows and orphans of those, who had fallen in the work, and for such preachers, as were on the superannuated list.

The house was crowded to its utmost capacity, and persons were passsng up and down the aisles, soliciting subscriptions, which, in an audible voice, with the name, were reported to the Secretary, on the platform. Fives and tens were offered freely for a while; but, by and by the tide ebbed, and it was only, "one dollar—Mr. Smith; one dollar—Mr. Jones, &c.," till at length, we were startled with the announcement—"$100! $100!" The Secretary called for the name. It was given—"Poor Sinner!" $100! "Wants the prayers of the Church." And many a hearty "Amen" went up, that he, who was so generously watering others, might be watered also, himself. I afterwards ascertained, that he gave $100 to some other benevolent object, and quite a sum to something else, making almost three hundred dollars, given by one, who did not make any pretensions to religion, and was a gambler by profession.

When asked, why he gave so freely and liberally, he said, it was a thank offering, for himself and family, for their preservation, while the pestilence was raging around them, and so many houses had been made desolate.

He had had no doctor's bill to pay. Not one of his family had been for a month, week, or day, on a sick bed; no loved eyelids closed in death, and he presented it freely, as a votive *offering of thanksgiving.*

In contrast, I will relate an instance, not only of great lack of *benevolence,* but may we not say, of *justice?*

Two preachers traveled a circuit, in Tennessee, containing 900 members, many of them wealthy farmers. One of these preachers was a married man; he received for his services $125. The other, a single man, received $31.50. Each had to find his own horse, and clothed himself. It was 300 miles around the circuit.

The young preacher traveled that year 3300 miles, laboring faithfully, and for all received $31.50. But he was as full of courage as ever, to start upon a new circuit for another year's labor. But the married man was obliged to locate. He could not support his family that way.

The people of that circuit, took few, or no religious papers, and would have been mortally offended, if a hint had been given, that they did not support their ministers faithfully.

CHAPTER XXV.

ANECDOTES OF THE CLERGY.

THE Clergy of any country or nation, will have a great influence upon the people, for good or evil. Why does New England stand head and shoulders above every other nation, that *now exists,* or has ever existed. In *morals, intelligence, industry, love of freedom, justice,* and everything, which relates to the *well being* of our *common humanity!* No one acquainted with our history, can deny, that the magic power of an intelligent and pious body of ministers, has had no little influence to bring about such *glorious results.*

We venture to say, that no two hundred years of the world's history, has ever exhibited, such an intelligent and exemplary body of men, so truly devoted to their work, viz: to advance the highest intellectual and moral improvement of the people.

All honor to them, in their high vocation. However Douglass and Border Ruffian Sympathizers may attempt to heap opprobrium upon them, for watching with such Argus eyes, against the encroachments of tyranny. The people, also, react and influence the clergy; and hence the Bible proverb—"Like people like priest."

The facts which I shall relate of the Clergy, will give some idea, of what the state of society must be, to allow such things.

A minister in Mississippi, got into a controversy with a Doctor of his congregation, concerning a small trade, about some damaged corn. From words, they proceeded to blows, the minister seizing a club, and the Doctor drawing his bowie knife. They were parted, however, by friends, before fatal results had taken place. But no charges were ever preferred against the minister, for conduct, not in accordance with his profession.

There was a preacher, by the name of ———, in Florida, a somewhat eccentric, but most *successful* laborer. Such a revival followed his labors, as the village had never seen. One of the subjects of it, was one of the most intelligent men in the place, a Doctor, a noted duellist. He was *so* skilled in the use of his six shooters, that it was sure death, with whomsoever he fought.

A difficulty sprang up between him and the minister. It was finally settled without bloodshed. But a local preacher, a member of the Quarterly Conference, told me that he expected nothing less, than that in some of their stormy, official meetings, blood would flow. The preacher always came armed with a loaded whip. And often, in his excitement, would jump to his feet, and with fierce language, shake his fists in the Doctor's face, who, though a dancing, drinking, fighting duelist, showed less of temper, than the minister, giving evidence, that the grace of God had been exercised on his heart.

This fighting parson, used to tell his people, "That if the devil should once get so completely into him, as to lead him to begin to *fight*, the one opposed, had better have his will made, and all earthly affairs closed up."

As a specimen of his plain manner of dealing with the people, I will relate an incident. Under one of his sermons, a well known slave woman, of undoubted piety, became exceedingly happy, and shouted aloud the high praises of God.

Some of the aristocratic, white ladies of the church were for having her silenced, and pnt out. And one of them arose and did so. This outrage, upon what the preacher felt to be, *religious liberty*, aroused his *fiery zeal*, and he poured out a most withering rebuke, in scorching, burning words, which so overpowered the white woman, that put her out, that she sank on the floor, to escape observation, and get out of sight.

He assured them, "that such Christian slaves, would be shouting in heaven, while they would be screaming for drops of water in hell."

It was not to be expected, that such plain dealing as that, would suit aristocratic slave holders, born to *rule*, and not to be rebuked. Trouble sprang up; and the faithful pastor, found the fire burning so fiercely around him, that he was obliged to leave. And as he did so, he said, "he would rather go to work, and help pave hell, with light wood knots, (pitch pine) than preach the gospel any longer, to the sinners in ———."

There was one of the most distinguished members of the ———, who, having found a lady that pleased him, had so far paid attentions, and secured her affections, that he thought the prize was surely his; and in the fulness of his joy, introduced her to a particular friend, who was so struck with her beauty, and the value of the prize, that the made attempts to supplant his friend, and win her for himself. And he succeeded, she having a rich vein of flirtation in her nature.

He felt it was a wrong, too deep to be passed over in silence, and sent him a challenge to fight. It was accepted, and the result was, only a shattered right hand on the part of the minister.

It is my opinion, after some reflection, that the lady was not worth risking life for, in this way.

It reminds one of an incident in the history of the Puritans. The brave Capt. Miles Standish, sending by the handsome John Alden, proposals of marriage to Miss Priscilla Mullins. She hints to the bearer, that he had only to make a similar offer, aud the valiant old Captain would have to look somewhere else for a bride.

A member of the ——— Conference, fought a duel. All right—he showed that he was a man of courage.

There has been much said of late, in some quarters, about the fighting clergy of New England, and of the propriety of their recommending, "Sharpe's Rifles," to those of their congregations, and others, who were about to make a home on the flower enameled prairies of Kanzas. While we would by no means deny, but that the old Revolutionary blood flows freely in their veins, and when it is necessary, to defend a great principle, they are ready to seize either the pen, or the sword, as circumstances may demand; yet, for a true fighting clergy, we think the North and East, must yield the palm to the South.

In that country, it is very common for different denominations, to unite in building the church, and then each occupy it, in a friendly way, as preachers, of different orders, may happen along; some days, having two or three sermons, and then weeks may pass by, without any.

At one of these churches, in Georgia, a Baptist lead off in the first sermon. He was followed by a Methodist brother, who scored the Baptist brother, and his doctrines, awfully. Another Baptist preacher was present, who was expected to give the third sermon. He arose at the proper time, and said, "That he felt much more like *fighting*, than he did like *preaching*, and that he could hardly find grace enough, to restrain himself from pitching his Methodist brother out of the window." And as he was a giant in strengh and size, weighing about two hundred, the Methodist brother was sorely frightened, lest he might, "*fall from grace*," and actually do it.

A very intelligent colored man, in Washington,

told me the following incident, which occurred the Sabbath before.

The Sacrament of the Lord's Supper was administered. At the South, the custom is, for the blacks, to partake after the whites. In some places, the colored are seated behind the whites; in others, they come and kneel at the altar after them. Sometimes, they remain in the gallery and are served by colored deacons. In the case I refer to, they all came and knelt at the altar.

As an aged colored Mother in Israel, of established christian character, had gained the vestibule, from the back part of the gallery, to take her place at the table of her Lord, she met the preacher passing out, all gloved, with hat in hand. He addressed her,

"Well, Milly, you must excuse me; I am invited to dinner, up at Mr. Corcoran's, (the great government banker, in W.) I fear I shall be late. You must go in and help yourself, and cover up the things nicely, when you are through."

My informant added, with true Afric wit, "that in his opinion, when the minister was in Mr. Corcoran's splendid parlor, it would be about as near heaven, as he would ever get."

Notwithstanding these facts, let it not, for a moment, be supposed, that the South has not in her pulpits, many men of self sacrifice, learning and devotion, who are an honor to their profession, and are doing good service for their Lord and Master. There is a readiness to *do*, and to *suffer*, which might not be equalled in the North and East. One fact, I will mention.

There appeared at the Memphis Conference, a brother from Louisiana, asking help from the older Conference, for the work, eight hundred miles south, which was so rapidly enlarging on their hands. He was invited to the platform, to make a statement of the wants of the people, whom he represented. And a more thrilling speech, it has seldom been my lot to hear.

The country, as he described it, was surpassingly beautiful. It was one eternal spring, where flowers never fade, and the air ever vocal with the song of birds. Those sudden changes of temperature, to which our northern clime is subject, bringing the seeds of death to so many, added to those terrible storms of rain, hail and snow, which here have undisputed sway, for six months in the year, are there unknown. He set forth the anxious desire of the Creole population, to hear the gospel, traveling from twenty to thirty miles, to listen to a single sermon.

He spoke of their willingness to support the institutions of religion; a starving salary was not to be collected, with great effort, by a dollar here, and another there, but single, large hearted, wealthy individuals, would pay the whole, and board the preacher, into the bargain. Others would build a good church from their own private funds. The people were hospitable in the highest degree, ready to do everything to make the preacher happy and contented among them.

There was one thing, however, of which he must forewarn them—the pestilence, the yellow fever, was but a too frequent visitant of their otherwise most inviting country. And when it came, though others might flee, the preacher *must not;* but laying aside his preaching, he must be at once, physician, and nurse, for both body and soul. Night and day, with little of rest and sleep, he must move among the dying and the dead, expecting every moment, when the condition and fate of others, shall be his own.

He would not conceal the fact, that in that very season, many a faithful ambassador of Jesus Christ, had fallen at his post. He wished their places supplied, as well as new fields of labor occupied. He would have them count the cost, realizing they would be called to witness such scenes of suffering and death, as were unknown among the green hills of Tennessee. But for the sake of perishing souls, he hoped the Macedonian cry of the people would be heard.

Volunteers were called for. Some ten, or more, gave in their names, that without going home, to bid wife or parents farewell, with horses ready bridled at the door, like the Light Brigade, at the terrible battle of Balaklava, they were ready, at the word, to charge some eight hundred miles down the river, into that valley of sin and moral death.

CHAPTER XXVI.

THE IGNORANCE OF THE SOUTH.

WE can only glance at some of its developments.

First, that they do not see how antagonistic, the system of Slavery is with the genius and spirit of our free institutions, or that they can flourish, side by side, together, instead of one or the other being driven to the wall, and crushed out. No one can write in favor of Slavery, without denying those self-evident propositions, contained in the, Declaration of Independence, "that all men are created free and equal." And Slavery propagandists both North and South, now boldly give the lie direct, to those great truths, uttered by the fathers of the revolution. If the people should believe in this Southern doctrine of tyrants, then would liberty be stabbed to the heart.

Secondly, their ignorance is seen, in that they suppose that Slavery, a relic of barbarism, can live, with the whole moral force of the civilized and christian world arrayed against it. They have yet to learn, that public opinion rules the world, and not the lash, or bayonets. It matters not, though for a time, this or that side seems to predominate, and obtains a great victory; in the end, public opinion wins the day.

Such a paper as the, "New York Tribune," the "Independent," and others that might be named, have more power, than an army of an hundred thousand men. Such an age of progress as this, of railroads, telegraphs, steamboats, printing presses, must work the death of this old and effete institution. And the sooner they make preparations for its burial, the better.

Again, their ignorance is seen, in that they seem not to know, what great and mighty results have been wrought out by free labor, when used side by side with slave.

The Free States, blooming like the garden of the Lord, covered with cities, villages, and the spacious dwellings of a prosperous people. While the vast forests, the rude log cabin, the unworked roads, the unbridged streams, the desolate appearance of things generally, in slave land, strikes the traveler from the Free States, with the greatest astonishment.

They seem to have no true idea, of the extent of our commerce, manufactures, or agriculture, and of the wealth, which is the natural result, of nourishing these branches of industry together. But they have the most preposterous ideas of the value of their great staple, *cotton*. To hear them talk, one would

think, they supposed the earth would cease to move, the sun would stand still in mid heaven, and the Free States starve to death generally, if they should cease to grow cotton.

They seem honestly to think, that they support the North, and if they should see fit to dissolve the Union, we should be ruined past hope. Our ships would rot at their wharves, and grass grow in the streets of our great cities. It was one universal declaration to me, throughout the South, "that unless we ceased to agitate the Slavery question, and silence those presses, which now plead so powerfully the rights of man, they must dissolve partnerships with us, and leave us to that destruction, which our crimes so justly deserved.

It seemed impossible for them to realize, that the dissolution of the Union, would be their *certain death*; but have no disastrous influence on us. And that every school boy laughs at this impotent and stale threat. They do not know, that the North has all the elements of prosperity within herself, and has nothing to fear from within or without.

There is, probably, no State in the Union, so highly favored in respect to harbors, navigable rivers, climate, fertility of the soil, mines of coal, copper, lead, gypsum, and even gold, as Virginia. No State so abounding with water privileges. Nothing but the curse of Slavery hinders her from becoming the leading State in the Union. But by being willing to hug this viper to her bosom, she must be contented with a place in the fourth or fifth rank.

Hear what one of her editors (Lynchburg, Virginia,) says, when speaking of her dependence, and the other Southern States, on the outside barbarous, upon those not favored with the social institutions of Slavery:

"Dependent upon Europe and the North, for almost every yard of cloth, and every coat, and boot, and hat we wear, for our axes, scythes, tubs, and buckets,—in short, for every thing except our bread and meat! It must occur to the South that if our relations with the North should ever be severed, and how soon they may be, none can know, (may God avert it long!) we would, in all the South, not be able to clothe ourselves. We could not fell our forests, plow our fields, nor mow our meadows. In fact, we would be reduced to a state more abject than we are willing to look at, even prospectively. And yet, with all these things staring us in the face, we shut our eyes, and go on blindfold."

The following quotation from the New Orleans Crescent, hints at the weakness of the South. Much stronger language might truthfully be used:

"We don't raise food enough to feed ourselves; we don't manufacture clothing enough to clothe ourselves; we don't keep the workshops of the world alive, have very few workshops of our own, and are obliged to depend upon foreign "workshops" for an infinite variety of indispensable articles; we have no ships of our own, yet we maintain in profitable employment, whole fleets of Northern and foreign vessels; we possess learned and able writers, yet the pen and ink with which they write, and the paper upon which they write, comes from foreign States; our newspapers will compare favorably with the newspapers of any other section, yet the types, presses, ink, and everything else, come from the North; we pride ourselves upon our fine horses, yet the saddles, bridles, martingales, harness, &c., with which those horses are caprisoned, in ninety-nine cases out of a hundred, are of Northern manufacture; we like to ride in fine carriages, and by patronizing Northern industry almost exclusively, check the growth of home industry; our immediate exports pay for the imports of the whole country, and regulate the exchanges of the earth, yet we, by ignoring the lessons common sense teaches, allow others to bear off the principal prizes in the grand commercial lottery; we are not silent in regard to our strength and prowess, or ability to do our enemies harm, yet we have few foundries for the manufacture of arms, depend for supplies of rifles, powder, shot, and percussion caps, upon others; have no cannon foundries, no powder manufacturing establishments, and, in fact, have nothing, literally nothing, whereby our people could vindicate their rights in case of an armed struggle! These facts may be homely, but they are none the less indisputable, and none the less worthy the consideration of practical statesmen."

Strange as it may seem, the South are in entire ignorance of the pecuniary loss they suffer by the institution. Any amount of testimony might be brought forward, to show, that under ordinary circumstances, the slave does not accomplish more than half as much labor as a free man. I saw many families paying from two to three hundred dollars a year for their servants, when seventy-five dollars, with us, would have furnished better help, and the board of one person saved, and many other etceteras.

Homer uttered a great truth when he said:

> " Jove fixed it certain, that whatever day,
> Makes man a slave, takes half his worth away."

If one man has one hundred, or five hundred slaves, toiling for him without wages, it may make him rich, but the wealth of the country, and its taxable property is not increased, as if each was a free man, toiling unceasingly to secure a competency for himself.

Again, the majority of them are in entire ignorance of the rapid spread of abolition sentiments in the Free States. The world has moved on, during the last twenty-five years, but they have not realized it. At the beginning of that period, a mob could be raised as easily to break up an abolition meeting, in any of the Free States, as to lynch an abolitionist now in the South. But all is changed. Few can be found, who do not profess to be opposed to Slavery.

In the last Presidental election, Freedom and Slavery met face to face, and in the next contest, there can be no doubt, which party will be victorious. They, at the South, good easy souls, have been sleeping over a volcano. They thought the North, at the command of Webster, would, "conquer their prejudices" on this, question of the age. When all the while, their hatred to Slavery, was becoming more and more intense. The South seem to be in entire ignorance of that terrible fate, which is approaching with a step, steady as Time, when the increase of the slaves shall have made them the dominant, or strongest party. They are making no efforts to arrest the terrible catastrophe, which the birth of every slave only renders more certain. They do not understand the great law of retribution, viz: that we cannot put a chain around the neck of another, but that one end of it, will clasp us in its terrible embrace. The slaves can not be held in a state of ignorance, and semi-barbarism, but that the whites must share, to a certain extent, the same fate.

It is an old proverb, verified by every day's experience, "that no man can do an injury to another, without receiving the butt end of it himself."

Of the hundreds of thousands at the South, that can neither read or write, have not the first elements of a common education, I need not speak. The census reveals most startling facts, they are known to all. To hear the hot heads of some, in South Carolina, talk, one would suppose their State, in men and material strength, was the banner State of the Union. While, by her own showing, she could not bring into the field, fifty thousand fighting men. While the old Bay State could muster two hundred thousand. And by means of her perfect net work of telegraphs, and railroads, could pour them, like a mighty avalanche, at a few hour's notice, on any rood of ground in her territory, where the enemy might be about to unfurl his banner.

CHAPTER XXVII.

SLAVE HOLDING FOR THE GLORY OF GOD.

We have at the North, a peculiar class of men, strongly conservative, quite benevolent in their way, minds of such peculiar idiosyncratic formation, so unable, or unwilling to follow a great principle out to its extreme conclusions, or an argument to its legitimate result, that though opposed to slavery, as a system, they think there are many cases, in which a man may take from his poor neighbor, his hard earned wages, year after year, and God's glory be promoted thereby. They make distinctions, where the bible does not. They would not have ministers hold slaves, but *the laity may,* not being able to see, that the bible has but one rule of morals, for clergy or laymen. It gives to no person, whether high or low, the right to practice immorality.

The Southern M. E. Church, act consistently, in allowing all, from their Bishops to the poorest member, who can afford it, to be slaveholders. And truly, "consistency is a jewel."

The church has ever had too many in her ranks, standing on the shifting quicksands of political expediency, and not on the rock of God's eternal truth,—men not willing to follow a principle beyond the line of easy practicability. They make comfortable and large reservations for the weaknesses, prejudices, and self interest of poor human nature; and think it extravagant, and radical, to force one into the extremes of trial and sacrifice. If some dear right hand sin offend you—even endanger your soul's salvation, do not cut it off and cast it from you. That would be *radical,* going to extremes, and might be very *inconvenient.* Better nurse and mollify it, cover it with poultices, which for the time being, shall render it somewhat easy, though it does nothing to hinder the fatal gangrene from rapidly extending to the seat of life. Be careful how you follow a principle to its final result. But turn aside, into some by-way arbor of expediency, which invites you to rest at the foot of the hill of difficulty. Pursue the straight and narrow path of duty, till you come to a crisis—till you begin to feel the pressure of the great principle you have adopted; then make a sagacious and prudent detour to accommodate the weakness of the *inner man*. This half principle class of men, are ready to say, "That slavery, for the most part, is an evil—nay, a very evil thing; that this is true of it, in ninety cases out of a hundred." This is as far as *public opinion* will now carry you. To go beyond this, would be very impolitic and dangerous to a man's popularity. Never think, or presume to stamp, the whole centre and circumference of slavery, with the burning brand of sin. Leave a thin luminous ring of righteousness, faintly glimmering, around this relic of Barbarism. "Spare, O, spare, to this huge, black iniquity, a few instances in a thousand, in which a man may hold another as a slave, or in other words, withhold from him, the reward of his labor, and still do so for the glory of God, and the honor of his justice and righteousness.

"As you value your popularity, do not go any farther; for in the catechism of expediency we are taught, that there is a diverging around extraordinary cases of difficulty, at the extreme end of a great principle. Let there be a few *extreme cases* to nestle, *Ruth-like*, under the white and flowing robe of the love and benevolence of God."

Men who use such language, are a very large and respectable class in the community. They may be very sincere. But it is easy to show, that all who are thus standing on the quicksands of expediency, must *sink*, and be submerged, when the battle is pushed to the gates.

The strongest man in the strength of this world, and the wisest in its wisdom, is powerless and guideless, unless he can plant his foot on the solid rock of a fixed principle, enunciated in God's word.

Whole principles bridge the abyss that separate time from eternity. Half principles are rafts, abutted on neither shore, bearing downwards those who stand upon them, to a gulf more to be feared, than that which receives the rushing cataract of Niagara.

Go with all the power of eloquence of this half principle preaching, or reasoning, and address the slaveholder, and see if you can make his conscience quake and tremble, with the conviction, that he is sinning against God, and endangering his soul's salvation. Speak boldly and fearlessly to him, and he will respect you all the more. Range before his eyes, like so many ghosts, its cruelties, sin and shame—the countless multitude of its thick set villainies.

Wax as warm and eloquent as the subject demands. Put the whole territory of slavery under the curse of God's law, with the exception of one rood's space; and see if every slaveholder in the land will not retreat to that standing ground, and find it wide enough, and safe enough, for the working of the inhuman institution.

Exempt from the ban, but *one instance*, in which, out of pure benevolence, and for the glory of God, a Bishop, Priest, or laymen, might hold a person, as a slave, and be guiltless; and then see, if every bloody Legree of the South, with his hands reeking with the blood of murdered Uncle Toms, and the withering, burning curses, of demented and crazy Cassys ringing in his ear, would not retreat to that same platform, and stand up equally as straight.

They ever affirmed to me, in all the States, that

they hold the slaves in bondage, out of *pure benevolence*, for the *best good* of the race, for the *highest interests* of humanity. To keep the negroes from becoming as wretched and miserable, as those of their own color in the Free States.

Householders there, will expatiate, with the greatest eloquence, on the difficulties of the system, and prove over and again, what trials of patience they have with these miserable beings, thrown upon their care. Or, as we should say, would be miserable, were it not for the merciful institution of slavery, which God's great goodness, has kindly provided for the colored race.

All therefore, at the North, who plead for benevolent slaveholding, are, unconsciously, perhaps, adding buttresses to the institution.

When we realize, however, what efforts they at the South make, to get those into their power, who escape, are willing to relieve their masters of this trouble and care, we can hardly give them credit, for all the disinterested benevolence they claim for themselves.

From our knowledge of human nature, we are inclined to think, that the assertion was true, made by an Episcopal minister, himself a slaveholder, to a company of clergymen, in the saloon of the Coosa Belle, on the Alabama river, when this subject was under consideration, viz: "Selfishness! selfishness! is at the bottom of the whole system. It is profitable for us, and therefore we continue it."

He ridiculed the sophistry of those, who would convince the North, that it is a great industrial, civilizing, educational system, having the highest interest of the colored man in view.

So far is true, that however benevolent a person may wish to have his particular slaveholding considered, every one that holds slaves, gives *so much* countenance to the system, as his example affords. If every holder was a real Legree, Slavery could not live a day. Such monsters live, and are sustained by the capital furnished, and strength given to the system, by a very different class of men—men that have many noble and excellent qualities.

www.ingramcontent.com/pod-product-compliance
Lightning Source LLC
LaVergne TN
LVHW021419110826
845150LV00007B/1995

* 9 7 8 1 4 2 5 5 0 8 8 5 2 *